EDUCATION LIBRARY
UNIVERSITY OF KENTUCKY

College Student Voices on Educational Reform

DOI: 10.1057/9781137351845

Other Palgrave Pivot titles

Raphael Sassower: **Digital Exposure: Postmodern Postcapitalism**

Peter Taylor-Gooby: **The Double Crisis of the Welfare State and What We Can Do About It**

Jeffrey Meyers: **Remembering Iris Murdoch: Letter and Interviews**

Grace Ji-Sun Kim: **Colonialism, *Han*, and the Transformative Spirit**

Rodanthi Tzanelli: **Olympic Ceremonialism and the Performance of National Character: From London 2012 to Rio 2016**

Marvin L Astrada and Félix E. Martín: **Russia and Latin America: From Nation-State to Society of States**

Ramin Jahanbegloo: **Democracy in Iran**

Mark Chou: **Theorising Democide: Why and How Democracies Fail**

David Levine: **Pathology of the Capitalist Spirit: An Essay on Greed, Hope, and Loss**

G. Douglas Atkins: **Alexander Pope's Catholic Vision: "Slave to No Sect"**

Frank Furedi: **Moral Crusades in an Age of Mistrust: The Jimmy Savile Scandal**

Edward J. Carvalho: **Puerto Rico Is in the Heart: Emigration, Labor, and Politics in the Life and Work of Frank Espada**

Peter Taylor-Gooby: **The Double Crisis of the Welfare State and What We Can Do About It**

Clayton D. Drinko: **Theatrical Improvisation, Consciousness, and Cognition**

Robert T. Tally Jr.: **Utopia in the Age of Globalization: Space, Representation, and the World System**

Benno Torgler and Marco Piatti: **A Century of *American Economic Review*: Insights on Critical Factors in Journal Publishing**

Asha Sen: **Postcolonial Yearning: Reshaping Spiritual and Secular Discourses in Contemporary Literature**

Maria-Ionela Neagu: **Decoding Political Discourse: Conceptual Metaphors and Argumentation**

Ralf Emmers: **Resource Management and Contested Territories in East Asia**

Peter Conn: **Adoption: A Brief Social and Cultural History**

Niranjan Ramakrishnan: **Reading Gandhi in the Twenty-First Century**

Joel Gwynne: **Erotic Memoirs and Postfeminism: The Politics of Pleasure**

Ira Nadel: **Modernism's Second Act: A Cultural Narrative**

Andy Sumner and Richard Mallett: **The Future of Foreign Aid: Development Cooperation and the New Geography of Global Poverty**

Tariq Mukhimer: **Hamas Rule in Gaza: Human Rights under Constraint**

Khen Lampert: **Meritocratic Education and Social Worthlessness**

G. Douglas Atkins: **Swift's Satires on Modernism: Battlegrounds of Reading and Writing**

David Schultz: **American Politics in the Age of Ignorance: Why Lawmakers Choose Belief over Research**

G. Douglas Atkins: **T.S. Eliot Materialized: Literal Meaning and Embodied Truth**

Martin Barker: **Live To Your Local Cinema: The Remarkable Rise of Livecasting**

DOI: 10.1057/9781137351845

palgrave▸pivot

College Student Voices on Educational Reform: Challenging and Changing Conversations

Edited by

Kevin J. Burke

Brian S Collier

Maria K. McKenna

DOI: 10.1057/9781137351845

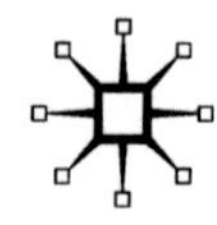

COLLEGE STUDENT VOICES ON EDUCATIONAL REFORM
Copyright © Kevin J. Burke, Brian S Collier, Maria K. McKenna, 2013.

All rights reserved.

First published in 2013 by
PALGRAVE MACMILLAN®
in the United States—a division of St. Martin's Press LLC,
175 Fifth Avenue, New York, NY 10010.

Where this book is distributed in the UK, Europe and the rest of the world, this is by Palgrave Macmillan, a division of Macmillan Publishers Limited, registered in England, company number 785998, of Houndmills, Basingstoke, Hampshire RG21 6XS.

Palgrave Macmillan is the global academic imprint of the above companies and has companies and representatives throughout the world.

Palgrave® and Macmillan® are registered trademarks in the United States, the United Kingdom, Europe and other countries.

ISBN: 978–1–137–35400–6 EPUB
ISBN: 978–1–137–35184–5 PDF
ISBN: 978–1–137–34303–1 Hardback

Library of Congress Cataloging-in-Publication Data is available from the Library of Congress.

A catalogue record of the book is available from the British Library.

First edition: 2013

www.palgrave.com/pivot

DOI: 10.1057/9781137351845

Educ.
LB
2165
.C65
2013

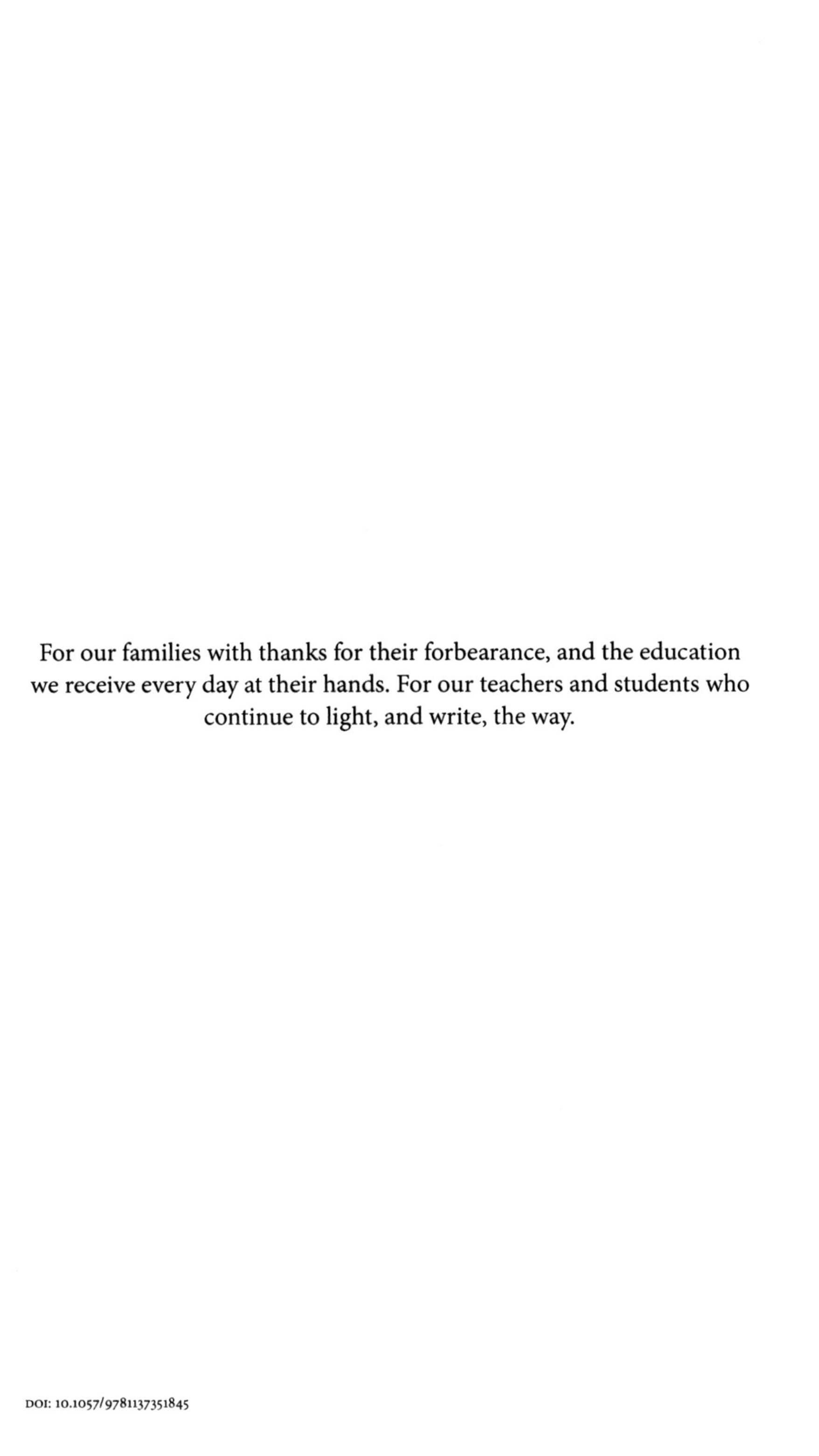

For our families with thanks for their forbearance, and the education we receive every day at their hands. For our teachers and students who continue to light, and write, the way.

DOI: 10.1057/9781137351845

Contents

Acknowledgments viii

Notes on Contributors ix

1 Introduction: A "Conversation" and the Problem of Positioning 1
Brian S Collier, Maria K. McKenna, and Kevin J. Burke

2 An Editorial Intervention: Mushfaking 29
Kevin J. Burke, Brian S Collier, and Maria K. McKenna

3 Literacy: Fostering Lifelong Learning 33
David Berton Grau, Kathleen B. Mullins, and Katherine A. Puszka with Kevin J. Burke

4 Early Childhood Education 53
Kathleen Buehler, Kelsie Corriston, Emily Franz, Meredith Holland, Allison Marchesani, and Maggie O'Brien with Maria K. McKenna

DOI: 10.1057/9781137351845

5 **The School Environment: Common Purpose in Separate Spaces** **79**
Carly Anderson, Sarah Cole, Kevin de la Montaigne, Sheila Keefe, Mary Claire O'Donnell, Casey Quinlan, Mary Clare Rigali, and Michael Savage with Brian S Collier

6 **Pulling Ideas Apart: Complicating the Questions** **105**
Maria K. McKenna, Kevin J. Burke, and Brian S Collier with Jessica Millen

Index **126**

DOI: 10.1057/9781137351845

Acknowledgments

We would like to thank, first and foremost, the students of the Education, Schooling and Society program at the University of Notre Dame not only for their influence on our pedagogy, but particularly for their work in helping us get hopeful about the future of teaching and research in the United States. Special thanks are in order to Stuart Greene for his ongoing support of this project, and all of our other projects; you have been an intellectual and emotional touchstone through our collective time with the program. Thanks, as well, to Julie Dallavis for her flexibility with and care for our students as they maneuvered in and out of our System course and thanks to Nancy McAdams for help in creating the course as we imagined it. And particularly, thank you to all of the students who persisted through the semester and full-year version of this experiment; it could not have been easy to muddle through with us and we are encouraged by your perseverance and long-standing good will. As ever, thanks to Amy, Lauren and Mark for their immense patience and quick wit.

DOI: 10.1057/9781137351845

Notes on Contributors

Kevin J. Burke holds a PhD in Curriculum, Teaching, and Educational Policy from Michigan State University. His interests center on curriculum theory and teacher education, most particularly the ways in which gender and religion come to in/re/deform student possibility and teacher training. His first book, *Masculinities and Other Hopeless Causes in an All-Boys Catholic School* (2011), is an autoethnographic examination of the discursive development of gender through the curriculum of religion.

Brian S Collier holds a PhD in History with a focus on American Indian Education from Arizona State University. His research centers on American Indian experiences in school and teacher education. Collier asks his students to think about ways that schools and people interact and how that shapes both culture and ways of knowing. Collier's other works focus on Catholic Indian Boarding Schools in the 20th century and American Indian running as community ceremony.

Maria K. McKenna holds a PhD in Educational Foundations from St. Louis University. Her research and teaching both focus on the ethic of educational care and minority experiences in American public education. Her work aims to pay particularly close attention to child and parent perspectives related to educational environments and opportunities. McKenna's work has been published in a variety of education related journals.

* * *

Carly Anderson is originally from Boston and graduated in the spring of 2012 from the University of Notre Dame, where she majored in History and minored in European Studies. Since graduation she has moved to New Haven, Connecticut, where she currently serves with AmeriCorps in an administrative position at a small Nativity Miguel middle school. As Graduate Support Coordinator, she works primarily with high school and college graduates, tracking and supporting them as they pursue college graduation.

David Berton Grau earned his B.A. from the University of Notre Dame in 2012. An Art History major, he dedicated his senior honors thesis to the study of 1st grade literacy instruction. Currently, he teaches 3rd and 4th grade science in Capitol Heights, Maryland, as a Teach for America corps member.

Kathleen Buehler of Pittsburgh, Pennsylvania, will graduate in 2013 with a B.A. in Marketing from the Mendoza College of Business, University of Notre Dame, and a cross-disciplinary minor in Education, Schooling, and Society. After graduation she plans to pursue a career in marketing while continuing to advocate for the safety of children and justice in the education system through various charities, including Marian Manor in Greentree, Pennsylvania, and Focus on Renewal in McKees Rocks, Pennsylvania, where she served as a pre-school teacher in 2010. While at Notre Dame, Kathleen pursued a variety of education research projects including statistical research and field research at a local elementary school.

Sarah Cole graduated from the University of Notre Dame in 2012 where she studied Management Consulting and Education, Schooling, and Society. She is originally from Scottsdale, Arizona but now resides in Chicago where she works as Technical Recruiter.

Kelsie Corriston is a Sociology major at the University of Notre Dame with minors in Education, Schooling, and Society and Italian Studies. After spending two summers doing educational service work, the first in Baltimore, Maryland, and the second in Komga, South Africa, she plans to pursue post-graduate service teaching.

Kevin de la Montaigne graduated from the University of Notre Dame in 2012 with a B.A. in American Studies. He is currently teaching writing and grammar to 5th through 8th graders at a Catholic elementary school in Tuscon, Arizona. While teaching, he is also pursuing a master's in education from the University of Notre Dame's Alliance for Catholic Education. Kevin

DOI: 10.1057/9781137351845

was most recently seen performing as Joseph in his school's Christmas concert, after an 8th grader was sidelined due to illness.

Emily Franz is a 2012 graduate of the University of Notre Dame. She holds a B.A. in Psychology and is currently a Teach for America corps member. She teaches 1st grade in St. Louis, Missouri.

Meredith Holland is a member of the University of Notre Dame Class of 2014, pursuing degrees in Economics and Theology. Meredith hopes to continue her studies of theology and education in graduate school, with a particular interest in Catholic higher education. In addition to her academic interests, Meredith is a member of the Notre Dame Folk Choir, co-President of the Notre Dame chapter of Students for Education Reform, and a volunteer at the Notre Dame Early Childhood Development Center.

Sheila Keefe graduated from the University of Notre Dame in 2012 with a B.A. in Economics and also completed a minor in Education, Schooling, and Society. She is currently teaching 3rd graders at a charter school on Chicago's South Side while pursuing a master's degree in elementary education at Northwestern University. Sheila has a "Learn Like a Champion" sign proudly hung at the front of her classroom and uses Notre Dame football statistics as the foundation for as many math word problems as possible.

Allison Marchesani is a 2012 graduate of Notre Dame where she studied Economics and Poverty Studies. She now works as a 2012 corps member with Teach for America, teaching high school mathematics in Indianapolis, Indiana.

Jessica Millen is a 2012 graduate from the University of Notre Dame where she majors in Sociology with a minor in Education, Schooling, and Society. At Notre Dame, she has conducted research on parent engagement and school desegregation. Upon graduation, she will be teaching elementary school in New Orleans, Louisiana with Teach for America. Following her two-year commitment, Jessica plans to go to graduate school and continue educational research.

Kathleen B. Mullins, originally from Hudson, Ohio, is a Film, Television, and Theatre major with a minor in Education, Schooling, and Society at the University of Notre Dame. After her graduation in 2014 she hopes to continue her proud advocacy for the arts by becoming a teacher and

DOI: 10.1057/9781137351845

enlivening and inspiring her students through the integration of performance in the classroom.

Maggie O'Brien is a member of the University of Notre Dame Class of 2014 and holds a minor in the Education, Schooling, and Society program. Originally from Milwaukee, Wisconsin, she is a member of the varsity cheerleading squad and works with the Notre Dame Vision program.

Mary Claire O'Donnell grew up in Boston and graduated in 2012 with a B.A. in Classics from the University of Notre Dame. Her love of children and learning helped propel her into a career in education through Teach for America. A 2012 corps member, Mary Claire is currently an English Language Learner resource teacher for kindergarten–2nd grade in Kansas City, Missouri.

Katherine A. Puszka is an English major, minoring in Education, Schooling, and Society at the University of Notre Dame. Katie, who is from Buffalo Grove, Illinois, will graduate in 2014. Upon graduation, she is interested in further exploring her passion for schooling and literacy acquisition by earning a masters in education and serving as a high school teacher.

Casey Quinlan was born and raised in Chicago and graduated with a B.A. in English and Spanish from the University of Notre Dame in May 2012. She studied in London and taught English to niños for a summer in a small village in rural Costa Rica, and thereby officially caught the travel bug. She now lives in Austin, Texas, where she is serving with the Jesuit Volunteer Corps as a case manager, volunteer co-ordinator, and general shelter-runner at a shelter for immigrant women and children experiencing homelessness.

Mary Clare Rigali is an Economics and Theology double major at the University of Notre Dame. She is originally from Santa Maria, California. Her time abroad in Santiago, Chile, has led to an interest in studying the role of Catholic education as it relates to economic development in Latin America. She is a member of the class of 2014.

Michael Savage is originally from the Chicagoland area. He is a current senior at the University of Notre Dame, where he studies Political Science and Africana Studies. After his graduation in May of 2013, Michael plans to attend law school.

DOI: 10.1057/9781137351845

1

Introduction: A "Conversation" and the Problem of Positioning

Brian S Collier, Maria K. McKenna, and Kevin J. Burke

Abstract: *What follows is a text about the ways in which purported experts come to define the parameters of what counts as a discussion around school reform. In order to fully situate the text that will follow—this book filled with student research and writing about how we might think about schooling in the United States—we will break this introduction chapter into three sections. The first seeks to situate the text in theory that aims to re-allow student voices into the process while also providing some description of the context for the student writing. The second examines the historical strands of our current system, suggesting that what we've lost is the public sense that the community is empowered to engage in educational policy debates. The final section will situate the text in the realm of pedagogy as we three seek to seriously think about the role of teaching and teachers in the realm of positing possibilities for education.*

Collier, Brian S, McKenna, Maria K. and Burke, Kevin J. *College Student Voices on Educational Reform: Challenging and Changing Conversations*. New York: Palgrave Macmillan, 2013. DOI: 10.1057/9781137351845.

Etymologically, the term "conversation" has two latinate origins, meaning roughly "with" (com) and "versus" (vertare). This is a bit of a loose and certainly ancient, if not antiquated, version of the word but the point to be carried here is that to converse, as in participating in a conversation, requires the very act of the word: "to turn about with" (*Oxford English Dictionary*—OED). That is, to be party to a conversation is to be active in putting forth ideas, but more importantly and more prominently as given in the Oxford English Dictionary, it requires an intimacy of engagement that can only come through "the action of living or having one's being in a place or among persons." And while we want to be careful to acknowledge the imperialistic history of the OED and its use as a creator and chronicler of certain kinds of histories (Willinsky, 1994), we see the use of definition here as a particularly salient way of suggesting first that language matters immensely in how it's leveraged for political purposes, but also to invite the reader into a very specific moment where students, as members of a year-long course, were given the chance to, with intimacy of purpose, "engage with things, in the way of business or study" to converse, for the sake of troubling certain waters.

To proceed, then, we must bring context to the conversation. In order to do so, however, another broader definition is necessary. The University of Notre Dame in an attempt to expand its role as a national and global research hub has, since 2006, designed and hosted year-long events structured around specific topics. This nearly annual series of events is meant to, presumably, create an environment of longitudinal study, punctuated with visiting scholars and experts, such that undergraduate and faculty engagement with broader social concerns is fostered, if not excited through various exchanges, events and ideally conversations. Topics tend to center on pressing social issues: in 2006 it was *The Global Health Crisis*; in 2007 it targeted immigration and after 2008s onus on sustainable energy the Forum, as it's called, turned to perhaps the most pressing of issues in the American consciousness on the heels of the mortgage-backed financial crisis: *The Global Marketplace and the Common Good*. This event, headlined by New York Times columnist Thomas Freidman marked a stark shift in the Forum, by our measure, from a broader engagement with ideas toward the promulgation of a very specific model for human possibility as marketized, commodified and reducible to some of the more dismal proclivities of economic scientificity/sophistry. This fed very readily into 2012s *Reimagining School*, which came to approach the notions of reform in the American context in rather, well, unimaginative ways. But more on that in a moment.

Back to definitions, quickly. A forum, as defined on the most recent iteration of the event's website, is "an assembly, meeting place for the discussion of questions of public interest" ("ND Forum," n.d.). This is important exactly because the university, by organizing a forum, is providing a space but not the terms for a genuine conversation. Were the series called the colloquy, literally a "talking together," then we might expect different things but this subtle move toward an emphasis on the place (as in, the university) rather than the topic itself comes to outline, we think, the kinds of talking that will happen.

It's important to note that our work in this text is not only about a series of meetings and supposed (or stunted) conversations at the University of Notre Dame. At the same time, it's not, not about this either as we are laden with a local context in our work. We exist in what Soja (1996) calls a "social space" which can, when conceptualized, "come to be seen entirely as mental space, an 'encrypted reality'" (p. 63). This is not to suggest that the physical place, this great schoolhouse, of the university doesn't exist but rather serves to shift the focus from the buildings in our Midwestern city onto the discourses produced by actors present within them, passing through them. Because "humans grow to maturity trained in the ways of such institutions" as our schools and colleges, we need to, in any critical project addressing education, attend to the ways in which this "training invariably depends on language of some sort" (Trites, 2000, p. 22). It is our intention to make claims that are larger than our own parochial situation, to move beyond our localized social space in order to engage in a critical study about how institutions come to position students—and where and how students in turn resist and reinvent such positioning—through official channels and the imposition of what Bakhtin (1994) calls authoritative discourse. Britzman (2003) notes that this discursive construct "demands allegiance" because it is "'received' and static knowledge, dispensed in a style that eludes the knower, but dictates, in some ways, the knower's frames of reference" (p. 42). We dig into, with the students in this text among other things, the limits of allegiance when demanded, implicitly and explicitly.

This book is, then, an examination of what happened when the concept of *Education Reform* became the topic of what could have been a discussion, a conversation, at our university over the course of a school year. It is about where authoritative discourse came to reign in the form

DOI: 10.1057/9781137351845

of an indoctrinatory approach to what is/was possible for K-12 schooling; more prominently this text, as produced by our undergraduate students, is an exercise in resistance and reconciliation. The essays included here are, we think, illustrative of the Bakhtinian "internally persuasive discourse" whereby student actors come to interpret and make non/sense of the messages promulgated through official university-sanctioned events around the topic of education reform. This is their work of "pulling...away from norms" toward "a variety of contradictory social discourses" (Britzman, 2003, p. 42) in the hopes of finding "newer ways to mean" (Bakhtin 1984, p. 346).

Alastair Pennycook (2001) argues that a critical applied linguistics will of necessity allow for a view of language "as productive and performative...as a set of repeated acts within a regulatory frame...and as a site of resistance to and appropriation of norms and forms of standardized discourse" (p. 168). What we propose here is a text underlined by these same values. It is our understanding that undergraduate students are often considered incomplete beings. They are good enough to enter our elite universities,[1] but they cannot, in some sense, be trusted with the production of big ideas, or real knowledge, so much as they can be easily positioned as consumers of them. They are not quite tabulae rasae but what they have to say and write is often seen at best as incomplete; at worst naïve and generally aimed at inflecting the expertise of those scholars to whom they are exposed or subjected to.

It is our sense that this explicitly anti-Deweyan (1902) approach to education where students are positioned as mere vessels for the prolixities of, and as parrots for, established "expert" positions is problematic and runs counter to the purpose of the university as a marketplace of ideas. With this assumption in place, we moved to create a dialogic space for student writing and scholarly work, accepting that, as Dejoy (2004) notes, "those who work to create different spaces for student subjectivities are worried about a different set of pedagogical, theoretical, and practical issues" (p. 50). We choose to examine this process (of discursive engagement with, resistance to, recapitulation of and research on writing and new subjectivities) through the latest iteration of the Notre Dame Forum, "Reimagining school: To nurture the soul of a nation"—which began in the spring of 2010 and continued through the spring of 2012—not because the ethos of the event was particularly unique, but specifically because we believe that it is representative of so much that happens on college campuses and particularly, of late, in reference to education policy.

DOI: 10.1057/9781137351845

Because we believe that "the strongest form of power may well be the ability to define social reality, to impose visions of the world" (Gal, as cited in Giroux, 2010, p. 59) and because the Forum was unofficially kicked off by an event entitled, "The system: Opportunity, crisis and obligation in K-12 education" and launched with posters and t-shirts emblazoned with the phrase, "we need to talk about this," it behooves us to think about who gets to talk and just what obligation and crisis mean and for whom. At a later event entitled "The conversation: Developing the schools our children deserve," a panel of prominent "leaders" in education suggested, once again, that this was something we might intimately share as a community, as we aimed to really "turn about with" the idea of schooling in the United States.

The point, of course, that was missing in the fanfare of these events and others was any public attempt to actually engage students in the kinds of intimate opportunities to really do the work of fostering the business of ideas about schooling. Instead, they were, when attending events, cast as audiences to the largely scripted speeches of prominent national figures who, though perhaps well versed in some aspects of the reform movement or the crisis of public schooling, such as it is or is seen, failed to, in any way, converse with students.

This text, produced in concert with a group of students who felt called not only to the place of the Forum but to the conversational aspect of its higher claims to truth, is meant to allow students to shift from being passive consumers to active producers of educational imaginaries.[2] It is, concurrently, a study of the processes of how such thinking and writing gets constructed by students as part of "a larger political project in which public intellectuals share a commitment to language as a site of experimentation, power, struggle and hope in the interests of building democratic social movements that are both inspired and informed" (Giroux, 2012, p. 100). The students have, in essence, written about education just as we have, but in different senses and spheres. To do so we will need to establish our frameworks more fully.

Framing

It is no stretch to suggest that our work together began with an aim toward developing the critical capacities of our students. That universities are politically positioned in the world is no surprise, really. When

DOI: 10.1057/9781137351845

these institutions, however, engage in heavily publicized forays into the public sphere—most particularly private universities—questions of how the town might be helped or harmed by the work of those hiding behind the gown are worth asking. That the conservative or liberal politics of a place might inform the list of guests invited to speak at events is, again, unsurprising. However, when such events which amount to stump speeches for, in this case, narrowly conceived neoliberal marketized "solutions" to a, in large part, invented "crisis" of American education are framed as conversations about topics rather than ideologically motivated screeds for and against certain stances within them, then the purpose of the university as a whole is, largely, compromised. Gone is the notion of the marketplace of ideas, that great agora where students and faculty barter freely amongst shiny new theories supporting and contravening each other but all the time in conversation and tension. And in its place we find the practice of the attempt at an active transfer of ideology under the guise of the more benevolent terminology of discussion. We do, indeed, need to talk about this but with the students, rather than at them.

We were, as faculty and scholars, concerned with the growing sense that students were mere set pieces to the machinations of an ideological (and foregone) set of speeches meant not so much to consider ideas as to impose them fully packaged and underquestioned. We are not entering into this project naively. We firmly believe that all curriculum, null, hidden and otherwise (Longstreet and Shane, 1992; Eisner, 1994), is of necessity ideologically saturated just as any educational project, because it purports to replace one kind of knowledge (or ignorance) with another, is on base, indoctrinatory. Rather, we wish to point to the ways that rhetoric and the framing of officialized events at a university become a generally untroubled part of "curriculum writ large" (Pinar, 2001, p. 32) at the intersections of the "embodied" students.

It was our emerging concern, as we attended the events promulgated under the umbrella of conversations and discussions, that what was occurring was the untroubled attempt at transferring ideology. It was as if the speakers at these events primed to talk with each other on stage, but never genuinely with students, were living "as if we were not there" in the kind of "absurd, paradoxical formula" that created the simulacra of a conversation where one never actually occurred (Baudrillard, 1994, p. 28). Students in the audiences of events were entreated, patronized and frozen, as the hope for the future of education reform but never

DOI: 10.1057/9781137351845

asked to engage in critical consideration for why reform was needed and whose version was best. Rather the audiences of these events were positioned (conditioned?) to accept what were exclusively "neoliberal policies of privatization and marketization" (Apple, 2012, xii) without question. Most disturbing were the moments when students, given the opportunity to speak with Forum participants in the public eye, were laughed off or evaded particularly when they suggested more nuanced and complex ways to read public education and the role of the public in/and private sectors.[3]

In answer to these concerns, then, we created a course aimed at fostering conversations that might best fall under the realm of Critical Social Theory (CST), "a multidisciplinary framework with the implicit goal of advancing the emancipatory function of knowledge" (Leonardo as cited in Watkins, 2012, p. 3). This CST approach is largely similar to the Freirean (1974) "critically transitive consciousness" characterized by "depth in the interpretation of problems" and "by the practice of dialogue" (p. 14). In honesty we didn't know quite what the students would say in answer to the Forum—some were and still are passionate advocates of charters and parental choice—but we wanted them to have the space to say it, to dialogue, to critique and to, ultimately, produce their own answers to the problems presented to them as already solved by the speakers they'd seen.

Contrary to traditional Marxist views of power, however, we don't see this work as simply that of an underclass of students resisting the strains of an overzealous administration, per say. Rather we wish to play with the nuances of language and the production of possibility and power through discourse(s). As such it will be important to elucidate two fundamental claims: first that we see much of the Forum as an exercise in curriculum where the underlying politics of reform become about "the concentrated expression of economics" (Watkins, 2012, p. 14) and are often obscured by the rhetoric of equal opportunity and individual choice. Further, as this is ultimately a project about the function of language and discourses in creating versions of the world, we note that "any discourse is defined not only by what it says, by the questions it raises, and by the actions it legitimates, but also by what it does not say, by the questions it cannot pose or answer, and by the actions it will not legitimize" (Foucault, 1980, p. 46).

What our former students have written in this text is about the authoritative discourses they have encountered in their lives and the ways they

DOI: 10.1057/9781137351845

have used internally persuasive techniques to make further sense of ideas, and this will always lead to partial and constrained versions of reality. This, we think, is all well and good as long as the claims made are mitigated by the notion that completeness is not the goal, but participation, creation and questioning are. And further what we were and are seeking is a genuineness and authenticity in conversation about education and, perhaps, reform largely found lacking in the staged events made available to students. Our understanding of the existential threat to an established order or narrative of genuine engagement with ideas is informed by the better angels of the Jesuit philosopher Bernard Lonergan, SJ (1997) who, all the same, suggests that a life and by turns a public discourse about vital issues must best be informed by a genuineness where:

> Genuineness is the admission of that tension—[between authenticity and falseness]—into consciousness... It does not brush questions aside, smother doubts, push problems down... It confronts issues, inspects them, studies their many aspects, works out their various Implications; contemplates their concrete consequences in one's own life and in the lives of others. (p. 261)

Our concerns, in writing portions of the text, are different from though certainly related to those topics, which the undergraduates have taken up. Though we envision ourselves as scholars of education and are thus intimately tied up in the implications of a policy and political drive such as that constituted by the winds of reform, our role in this book is not to write about specific initiatives or modes of teacher training, say, but rather to examine the process by which students came to be, in essence, literate in their own discursive power around the topic of educational reform. The students are writing of K-12 education reform; we are writing around and about the situations of their coming to write. We set out in the realms of theory, history and pedagogy to "explore the real stuff of literacy: conveying something meaningful, communicating information, creating narratives, shaping what [they] see and feel and believe into written language" (Rose, 1989, p. 109) as it tied to power and discourse and truth.

Foucault (1972) insists that a:

> will to truth, like the other systems of exclusion, relies on institutional support: it is both reinforced and accompanied by whole strata of practices such as pedagogy—naturally ... but it is probably even more profoundly accompanied by the manner in which knowledge is employed in a society, the way in which it is exploited, divided and, in some ways, attributed. (p. 219)

DOI: 10.1057/9781137351845

In this sense, then, we acknowledge that what is produced here by both our students and their professors is constrained, ever partial, in its claims to truths. We have, just as the organizers of the Forum did before us, come to define for our students what based on our own ideologies, hidden biases and explicit aims, will come to de/limit the "discursive relations" by which this project has been defined. And though these relations are for Foucault "at the limit of discourse" by "offering... objects of which" we and they can "speak" by "determin[ing] the group of relations that discourse must establish in order to speak of this or that object" (p. 46), we still see hope for the production of theory and research by undergraduates amidst this swirl of discursivity, authoritative, internally persuasive or otherwise.

Make no mistake, this is a critical project whereby the students set about to examine the often troubling (re)formation of education in the United States. We understand "critical here [as] a political critique and not merely a way of thinking" (Pennycook, 2001, p. 171). This then "allows us to view language as productive and performative" (p. 168) and also as a "site of resistance to the appropriation of norms and forms of standardized discourse" (p. 168). And of course thinking about standardized discourse or authoritative discourse or the political ministrations of a university forum which positions students as passive consumers must lead us to the ways we can conceptualize power. In answer to this we will defer to Foucault (1980), one final time, noting that "posing for discourse the question of power means basically to ask whom does discourse serve?" (p. 115).

Our hope for this text is that it engages the very real question of how the discursive functionality of university events—and any staged public events, really—in the appropriation of student "audiences" serves certain interests. Worsham (2002) distinguishes between "intellectual and academic work." The latter is "inherently conservative inasmuch as it seeks to fulfill the relatively narrow and policed goals... of a given profession" and, more to the point in the case we take up here with the Forum, in its service in fulfilling "the increasingly corporatized mission of higher [and any] education" (p. 101). Intellectual work seeks to, in this case, work with students to become "relentlessly critical, self-critical, and potentially revolutionary" (p. 101) in their widened scope for what is possible through scholarship, through school, through writing. To that end, we sought to foster, to borrow again from Worsham, the kind of passion that drives theory that becomes a "passion for questions, for a questioning attitude"

DOI: 10.1057/9781137351845

(p. 103) among our students, our writers such that the text itself became a kind of journey of remaking often prepackaged ideas rather than an end on its own. It will be up to the reader and the students to examine the "who" implicated within certain kinds of academic work-discourses and what that implicates in terms of power and, specifically, who gets served in the process of talking, but not conversing, about school reform. As a way of framing the conversation going forward we now turn to a brief and incomplete, though we think suggestive, history of schooling as forum and as reform(ed).

Historicizing the notion of reform

In thinking about the history of education too often people want to think about schools, meaning their (former or current) school. Legislators, presidents, city council people, and school board members all seem to deal with the idea of school as being the one that they've attended and as such are oft times working to create a system that can't possibly exist because, to quote *They Might Be Giants*, "time, it marches on and time, it still marches on." The idea of re-creating schools of the past is a fairly recent problem of nostalgia and largely a nostalgia for an American school system that really never existed. As people look to re-create their own schools they are quick to forget the problems that schools of the past presented for people who did not grow up to become policy analysts, legislators, or elected school board officials. In short, many people are working hard to re-create schools that were only imaginary to begin with and that's, well, hard to do. Instead of an imagined past educational system, we need to think about successful elements of what came before the present, and in part how we've arrived at the present. Vital to remember here, and going forward in this text, is the need to take a longer view of the concept of education reform; that is, since the beginning of schooling as a formalized concept, teachers, students and the curriculum of the schoolhouse have always been in reform. This is the nature of the term—literally to re-form something—but also of the dynamic interplay of policy, community desire and the vision of producing certain kinds of citizens.

When working with students we can quickly get to issues surrounding contemporary education by examining what each student in the course thinks the purpose of education might be. We are rarely able to

DOI: 10.1057/9781137351845

get any two students to say the exact same thing. This becomes even more problematic if we take this example outside of a university classroom and begin to ask parents from multiple demographics what they think the purpose of education or schooling is; some will talk about safety, some will talk about school as a community center, some will talk about it as a place to gain skills for a job, and others think of it as a place to gain access to the world beyond their own socioeconomic circumstances. The above, clearly, is not an exhaustive list either. So, as educators, politicians, families, policymakers and citizens we are left at the starting line not knowing where we are headed when it comes to ways of thinking about education and educational reform because as a community we've ceded our ability to speak about education or changes in education to non-practitioners and proxy lawmakers who make decisions by thinking through what is temporarily popular, and thus will help their career, instead of what is possible or considering what was successful in the past.

On the North American continent the first formal systems of education happened in communities with the idea that the education children received benefitted an entire community. To this end, community members were tasked with showing the young how things worked in society, other community members taught very specific history lessons many of which also taught citizenship and imbued children with a sense that they were part of a larger community and world. Other adults were tasked with teaching skills that would help the children survive and flourish. This system was highly organized and incredibly fluid at the same time. As community needs shifted or changed so too did the lessons that students received, and the whole community knew what lessons and pieces it needed and thus worked co-operatively to ensure the future of the community. Of course, this system of education was found in Indigenous communities in North America with nothing so recognizable as governmental oversight in a modern sense. A system of education that prepared people to care for themselves and others, taught people to farm and hunt, to cook and to share and an education that taught science, history, music, and culture. This entire system was governed by what the community needed and desired from its young people and the kids had good skills both because it was expected of them and because it was necessary, but also in many cases because the skills led them to more responsibilities and privileges. This incredibly effective leveled community-based system of education is likely, and perhaps ironically,

DOI: 10.1057/9781137351845

what we strive for as a modern American nation. However, we are destined to struggle as a people, perhaps in part for the sins of ignoring what was already effective and flourishing in educational pedagogy on this continent before it was altered by European ideas about education and its purpose. Of course, everything was not perfect for Native people all of the time in their educational systems, but a lesson can be learned from this as well—that while things may have been better in the past we can't romanticize the past either.

In some ways then, European contact becomes part of the first major educational reform in North America that's as yet documented. This educational reform began in fits and starts in the 16th century with the setting up of Spanish Missions in both Florida and present-day California. The idea that the first formal European educational institutions were the Missions is an important one to grasp. The Missions served multiple purposes for the Spanish who spent the 16th century busily exploring lands that they believed, upon "discovery," belonged to them. The first purpose was that of presidio or fortress. The Missions were in essence outposts that provided a place for military men and their parties to re-stock and rest between their forays into the new land. The second purpose of the Missions was religious. Likely the priests and brothers who ran and staffed the missions may have felt their own religious calling was primary; still the regular visitors who came to the Mission certainly saw and recognized the accouterments of force, particularly because to gain footing to build Missions people like Ponce De Leon, Álvar Nuñez Cabeza de Vaca, and Don Juan Oñate fired on and harmed Indigenous people (Entrada, 1994). As an extension of the religious element of the Missions came an educational element, but pedagogy, and often orthodoxy, went hand in hand with religion for Europeans and so this shift should not be at all surprising to those familiar with Judeo-Christian traditions. Assimilation by force and through education is not an uncommon story in educational accounts of Native people, in fact the US government is perhaps the most forward in showing that education can be an act of war, as the War Department paid for the first Indian Schools in the modern United States during President Grant's administration (Prucha, 1976; 1984).[4]

While the Spanish Missions clearly set-up a formal system of education it was not until the schools of colonial Massachusetts in 1642 and 1647 that formalized public education became commonplace in towns with over 50 residents. These parameters though are not unlike the

DOI: 10.1057/9781137351845

rationale for the founding of the Spanish Missions before. Indeed the 1647 Old Deluder Satan Law was used to establish schools for:

> It being one chief point of that old deluder, Satan, to keep men from the knowledge of Scriptures, as in former times, by keeping them in an unknown tongue, so in these latter times, by persuading them from the use of tongues that so at last the true sense and meaning of the original might be clouded by false glosses of saint-seeming deceivers, that learning might not be buried in the graves of our fathers, in church and commonwealth, the Lord assisting our endeavours,—it is therefore ordered. (as cited in Ward and Waller, 2000)

While there were likely other small town laws that preceded Old Deluder Satan, it is important to think of this law as one of the first texts that governed education and its American purpose. In essence the law serves as one of the important precedent-setting guidelines for schools and for education.

The idea of religion in schools is important, but also is the idea that communities believed that education was important to the existence of the community, so much so that any town breaking the law was fined. The fines were stiff penalties that eventually helped pay for the education that students would receive; moreover, the fines and the schools themselves became the story of how American schools would be funded by individual citizens through a community expense. It was generally understood that the whole town was going to pay for this education regardless of whether or not an individual had children who would benefit directly from the school. This is the basis for universal public schooling in this country. One might even argue that the Spanish were laying the groundwork for what would become the Catholic system where the Church pays for education, but in the public system, even though it has religion at its roots, the towns were and are compelled to pay to educate the masses.[5]

The early towns of 50 or more people had a problem however: they couldn't find enough qualified teachers to run their schools. Fairly regularly did the Ol' Deluder Satan act cost towns money because they just could not find anyone to teach. So from the very start of American education we have towns that wanted an educational reform, or that were at least willing to adhere to a law, but were hindered in doing so due to a teacher shortage. The point being that education, even in its most rudimentary forms, was hard to achieve.

DOI: 10.1057/9781137351845

The schoolhouse in community practice

The rooms that were used for schools in the colonial period also doubled as meeting halls for towns and even in some places worship halls. These rooms themselves held a magical quality for being the space in which American education, the harbinger of opportunity, existed. These schoolrooms were essentially places where public forums and ideas were created, where communities of interested parties came together to listen, learn, and most importantly discuss. These rooms were not only schoolrooms, they were the rooms where people came together from the populace to make educational policies for their communities. These schoolrooms exist in American myth as powerful images of an independent form of education and a successful building block of American thinking. They are, in turn, romanticized and popularized in American History textbooks and in American literature, giving these spaces a pedagogical power of their own. Americans regularly like to recall the one-room schoolhouse where John Adams taught in Worcester, Massachusetts. Americans are perhaps most familiar with the image of a young Abraham Lincoln being educated on the frontier in one-room schoolhouses and through his own moxie and desire to read. Perhaps most impressively in American popular imaginary image comes the one-room-schoolhouse that Laura Ingalls Wilder enshrined in her "Little House" books that were later adapted for television. The popular icon, we find, of American education then is the one-room-schoolhouse from which, in American mythology, if people work hard they can become anything they like. This myth is particularly powerful in the case of Abraham Lincoln's childhood story: as education, and school are to have saved a young mind on the frontier. Older generations in the American populace like these stories in part because we were raised on them in our own schools and there is a very specific vision of the school as a communal meeting place and the school as providing individual uplift.

Moving up

As the nation industrialized in the 19th century the need for education changed too. Ideas began to move more rapidly as the first American spellings were popularized by Noah Webster, and his American printing press helped to disseminate ideas in a new American version of the

DOI: 10.1057/9781137351845

English language. Ideas also travelled quickly as Americans moved to urban areas for work in the second half of the 19th century. As these citizens lived in urban places there was a great fear of rising crime rates and once again Americans thought about education, this time to help civilize the population.

Later, an underlying notion of education as social reform existed in the thinking of John Dewey, a thinking that was greatly influenced by his relationships with reformers who understood education and the need to transform from it (Deegan, 1988). Dewey thought that:

> The political and governmental phase of democracy is a means, the best means so far found, for realizing ends that lie in the wide domain of human relationships and the development of human personality...it seems to me, as the necessity for participation of every mature human being in formation of the values that regulate the living of men [sic] together; which is necessary from the standpoint of both the general social welfare and the full development of human beings as individuals. (1939, p. 400)

In Dewey's work here and elsewhere we see him striving to create a system that allows for social welfare and development of a society. It is this shift that Dewey thought about during his tenure in Massachusetts and developed during his time interacting with Jane Addams and the people she served, that became the basis for much of what we call educational pedagogy.

Also working in the arena of public education in the 19th century were the Lyceum lectures and the Chautauqua movement. In both cases speakers came to educate the masses as an addition to formalized education. These symposia would bring people who were well-known speakers to venues around the country to speak and help shape public sentiment or challenge ideas. It was not uncommon for speakers such as Elizabeth Cady Stanton, Susan B. Anthony, Frederick Douglas, Ralph Waldo Emerson, and Henry David Thoreau among other luminaries to be regularly requested speakers in these movements. The Lyceum and Chautauqua movements are the predecessors of the modern symposium or speaker series at contemporary American universities.

In the modern format speakers are often expected to discuss large ideas in 50 minutes with a few minutes left for questions and answers. And unlike the Lyceum movement the audience in the modern university seminar or guest speaker series is provided with little opportunity for dialogue and discussion. Considering educational roots in those

DOI: 10.1057/9781137351845

early schoolhouses and schoolrooms, certainly we ought examine the current format of non-discussion-based-lecture, which in the present we know can become a pedagogical tool aimed at the direct transfer or information. Audiences of American antiquity would vote for speakers and itinerant experts with their feet and their voices, but present-day decorum and a shift in tradition has disallowed discussions in useful and meaningful ways. There is, in particular, a compulsion (internal and enforced) at universities like ours that defines student involvement, often, by attendance at extracurricular events. Critical engagement with them is certainly another thing entirely.

All education has an agenda and in America that agenda shifts around regularly; as the nation has grown the agenda has allowed for middle-level policy managers, an incipient bureaucracy (Katz, 1987) dictating policy decisions in lieu of communal, discussion-based reform. As a nation we've ceded so called expertise in areas of education to politicians and non-practitioners without allowing for thoughtful discussion about who or what education needs to be, we've moved so far from the Native American model, or even the colonial or early American model, that we can no longer see that to work well, educational policy needs to have those involved in the process also involved in discussions about and around it.

So, again, we must ask: what is the purpose of education? Often we don't remember that the purpose of education is multifaceted, but even more often we forget to ask our students, or other constituent groups, this crucial question. In asking students their vision of the purpose(s) of education we begin to empower them to become future policy analysts, legislators, and elected school board officials or at the very least citizens who will no longer give tacit consent to an education system that operates in their name and perhaps at cross-purposes for the common good of their nation. Given the above history and relying on the assumption of a troubling shift in the ways in which education policy gets talked about, particularly thinking about who gets to be expert, we now move to a discussion of the pedagogical implications of education and particularly of this project and its writings.

Pedagogy and the learning process

Writing a book in which we are considering both the pedagogy of the undergraduate students with whom we are writing the book and the

DOI: 10.1057/9781137351845

pedagogy of schooling en masse might well cause confusion. However, the pedagogical considerations for these two groups, and others, are similar irrespective of who we are referring to because of the fundamental truth that learning is a dialogic process rooted in give and take. What's more, thinking through the relationships, content, methods, and environment of a learning process can be a productive meta-cognitive exercise. It is possible, as in the case of this text, that the undertaking becomes a public endeavor, whereby examining the conditions of learning from multiple perspectives allows a larger discussion on education to emerge. In choosing to examine micro- and macro-level examples of learning processes we intend to provoke conversation on the conditions which allow children (and adults) to come to their own understanding of a given idea; in our case, "what are lasting impactful interventions in schooling to improve learning processes writ large?"

To continue, we turn to pedagogy. Individuals who are privileged enough to have the position of teaching and who care to impact educational outcomes in ways that elicit meaningful learning as demonstrated through a commitment to civic duty, self improvement, self sufficiency, and attention to the common good must be watchful and cognizant of the changing terrain within the educational landscape. Educators, young and old, should be weary/wary of ideology and concerned with the way individual learning is valued over the collective. We must also consider the primacy of response to any given discourse that views teaching through an exponential lens. That is to say, in the ideal, the teaching of one begets the teaching of the many. In the case of our writing here, when students think deeply about the educational endeavor that our nation has committed itself to in word and deed (or any other topic for that matter) they must have the opportunity to challenge various facets of the enterprise precisely because of the power they hold as future voters, leaders, and educators. Without an opportunity to challenge dominant discourse, students (and faculty) are no longer being asked to learn, innovate, or create so much as to believe. If this becomes the norm, then this will most certainly point to a fundamental shift in the form and function of the Academy, read: education writ large, as we know it. Historically, we see trends in this direction throughout the United States but in particular in recent decades with the English-only movement, the ban of ethnic studies programs, and a consistent push for a narrower, nationalized, and dare we say, "whitewashed" curriculum.

DOI: 10.1057/9781137351845

We evoke Bakhtin's (1981) distinctions between persuasive (understanding arrived at through reflection, conversation, and commitment to ideas) and authoritative (knowledge with authority and demand for allegiance already attached) discourse in our writing alongside our students with an underlying belief that, "Primacy belongs to the response, as the activating principle: it creates the ground for understanding, it prepares the ground for an active and engaged understanding... Understanding comes to fruition only in the response" (p. 282). We assert that this book, while allowing students to consider a variety of facets of education, serves as a model of how layers of communication, co-operation, and understanding, specifically across lines of power and while attending to power differentials, in any undertaking can yield unexpected results, novel ideas, and a stronger, more persuasive foundation for belief sets and subsequent action. As authors, and academics, we are interested parties, both in the role this text plays in critical university studies and also in the discourses surrounding K-12 education. But in fact, while we do acknowledge the positionality of our role as professors to that of the students and understand that all language/knowledge is ideologically saturated we *do not* tacitly or explicitly demand our students' allegiance to any one idea set, political ideology, or process. At the outset of this endeavor, we asked for intellectual commitment and rigorous investigation of ideas—ours, theirs, and those of others. We believe this is not only our job but our moral responsibility as individuals in a position of relative power. Throughout this text you will see our collective struggle to adhere to this demand with varying degrees of success.

When approached about writing this book, students were skeptical. They questioned what they had to offer to the conversation about education. They wondered who would take them seriously. And they doubted they could do it. Three quarters of the way through our year-long course we were still working to convince the students that they had something valuable to say and write about education reform and policy. Moreover, we were still working to convince them that there was room for voices within the conversation. In those moments, we heard and saw, very literally, how important this undertaking was for all of us. We regularly saw the depth to which they believed that those labeled "experts" by unknown means knew better than they did. Perhaps most importantly, we learned that authoritative discourse was, in some ways, more comfortable and familiar to them than any other type of learning. They discussed the ways in which they were told what, when, and how to

DOI: 10.1057/9781137351845

study and how this class was so very, very different from any other they had experienced. We recognized the lack of empowerment and agency in authoritative discourses of their past educational experiences and regularly reiterated the depth to which we believed in the basic principle of all constituent voices needing to be heard in dialogue surrounding any, and all, democratic enterprise.

Learners big and small

When striving to fully understand some facet of life as learners we cannot divorce the practical from the philosophical, the sociological from the biological, nor the political from the historical. As Rorty (1979) reminds us, hermeneutical thinking requires conversation in which no pre-conceived disciplinary matrix dictates the outcome and dialogue is always a possibility. When we fail at the above, we are neither fully prepared to use knowledge nor are we able to pass that knowledge on to others in sufficient detail to spur on the creation and dissemination of new thinking. Understanding the interdisciplinarity of the learning process and the interconnectedness of the world is at the heart of deep understanding and meaningful learning. This understanding (that depth to learning matters) is at the core of what educational reformers, parents, and concerned citizens must continue to demand for our children but also demand from our policymakers, politicians, academicians, and school leaders. The creation of this text demanded something similar of our students and of us, challenging our very notions of what it meant to teach and learn.

Certainly, shallow learning exists, especially where discreet facts are involved in the K-12 world. In fact, much of this learning is necessary and precursory to bigger thinking; the definitions that a student crams into her head for a test the next morning, the statistics about this or that area of the country, a formula for completing a math assignment, even knowing the details of a new state law. However, it is incumbent upon all of us to remember that these facts do us little good when never placed in context or measured in the context of larger thinking, though ideas like these are often heralded as *the* measure of learning. Make no mistake: we understand that at the point of specialization in higher education, and even in limited instances in K-12 education, there is indisputably a place for factual learning. Students must have an opportunity to recognize the value of instances in disciplines, courses, and fields where this is the case,

DOI: 10.1057/9781137351845

but we must also make clear this is not the only way to understand and/or consume knowledge.

Our goal in looking critically at an academic enterprise and the content of that enterprise with students is a deep and forward thinking goal. Our hope is that learning through the creation of something new challenges existing paradigms or ideas of the writers and readers alike; making individuals sit in the uncomfortable realm of feeling like they know less at the end of the process than when they started. We and our students emphasize here that this type of learning is not only healthy but necessary for us as a human collective to move forward, heralding Britzman's (1998) work focused on the notion of *difficult knowledge*. Difficult knowledge—knowledge which is unknown, but then when introduced is resisted or only partially understood due to the magnitude or complexity of the content, particularly in the often uncomfortable implications it has for the consumer is a new type of knowledge for many a student (and instructor). We are told, if not necessarily taught, early on in the educative process that the goal is to be an "expert" not a "dilettante." Britzman insightfully lays out an alternative possibility with hope as a necessary corollary to difficult knowledge as a "means to an end" of understanding. It is through hope, she asserts, that individuals are able to first acknowledge difficult ideas but then successfully integrate them into their own consciousness. Contentedness with the status quo or routinely accepting that which is placed in front of us is, at times, a form of effortless complacency. In other cases, and perhaps the more worrisome condition to be concerned with, it is a benign or willful ignorance of an alternative reality where questioning is welcome, challenge is accepted, and disagreement expected about whatever discourse is inherently difficult.

Besides being comfortable with difficult knowledge we purport that teachers of any kind have an obligation to cultivate in students the desire to hope and therefore the desire to challenge ideas and knowledge. We have an obligation as educators to foster the motivation of students to connect ideas, and beg from each of them tolerance enough to examine personal and collegial thinking from a host of angles. To do this we must then consider all of the pedagogical tools at our disposal.

A study of more than 100 top college and university professors found that "best" teaching involved five unifying principles (Bain, 2004).[6] These principles all aim to create a *natural but critical* learning environment. According to Bain, an intriguing question or problem must undergird the successful learning process of any course or learning endeavor.

DOI: 10.1057/9781137351845

However, it is not enough to simply have the question. There must also be significant scaffolding and patience involved in helping students understand the importance of the question at hand. Students must be engaged in higher order processes and "*never* only to listen and remember" (p. 102, emphasis added). Lastly, students must come to their own solutions to the question presented which then begs them to be curious about the *next* question.

Learner tensions and paradoxes

As we approach the close of this section of the text we must address our learners and the fact that learning, where the goal is not indoctrination or forced subjugation, involves unavoidable tensions. These tensions reside internally and externally for the learner and are, in some ways, all-important; they signal the willingness of the learner to think and speak about the ways in which new ideas or information intersect and collide with existing understanding. As Bakhtin (1994) notes, speech is both expressive and evaluative. Our challenge remains that we avoid focusing so much on the first that we neglect to remember the second. In our minds, there is no question that the act of learning is a balance of acting and reacting, absorbing and producing, and knowing versus not knowing, believing and challenging. It is also an undertaking that requires a clarity of position from the vantage point of the learner. Unfortunately, this is not always the case, particularly when authoritative discourse is the dominant paradigm in which students and/or faculty are placed, as was the case in the Forum.

Research on various aspects of understanding inner discourse construction abounds in the disciplines of education, psychology, and communication. Vygotsky's (1962/1986) notion of internal speech construction prior to external verbalizations comes to mind. Similarly, Freud's (1949) links between behavior, instinct, and the subconscious are important to explore and consider. Taking this idea one step further, the moral, cultural, and/or religious filters of individuals clearly play a role in discursive construction and must be acknowledged as part of coming to know (Coles, 1986; Coles, 1990; Kohlberg, 1966). Our inner constructions of truth and fiction rest heavily on our lived experience and cultural milieu and we would do well to give space to these truths in conversations on learning.

DOI: 10.1057/9781137351845

In Goffman's (1959) classic, *The Presentation of Self in Everyday Life*, the reader is reminded that life is, in fact, akin to a constant performance. The depth to which we hold character, play a role, script a part for ourselves, or create a diversion or distraction from that which is most worrisome to us rings out in Goffman's work. This is never truer than in moments of learning regardless of setting. Our student co-authors have readily conveyed throughout this process their confusion about the "role" we have asked them to play as an "expert" as it disturbs the general equilibrium of their learning patterns in formal and informal contexts. Consider also Reiss' (2004) powerful work on intrinsic motivation and the 16 underlying needs that motivate individuals to act among them: power, curiosity, security, independence, social contact, honor, idealism, to name but a few. Reiss' research also carries with it a claim that the more religiously minded an individual is, the less the individual is intrinsically motivated by autonomy/autonomous thinking. This is especially powerful when considering that this book was authored, at least in part, by a group of 33 students, 90% of whom identify themselves as Catholic but where just fewer than half describe themselves as "people of faith."[7]

Positionality

Further consideration of a given individual's position as they come to "know" is essential to understanding as we work toward making explicit those facets of learning that are either implied or ignored depending on the circumstances. Tuan's (1977) explanation of positionality is valuable to circle back to in the text at this juncture. As we noted earlier in the chapter, market ideologies, capitalist structures, and the rhetoric of efficiency, excellence, and equity framed the Forum for the year. But as Suzanne Wilson noted in a recent campus lecture and in multiple conversations with students,[8] these terms—efficiency, excellence, and equity—are not universally understood and most definitely mean different things to different people. Tuan and Goffman remind us that, like communication, we are always making sense of physical and literal space and our evolving understanding of place in relation to others. This echoes Bakhtin's (1994) sentiments that we are unable to create persuasive discourse without the specific opportunity to share thoughts. And, as we continue to reiterate, positionality implies power, relationship, and hierarchical dynamics that cannot go unnoticed or unacknowledged. Tuan also reminds us of the

DOI: 10.1057/9781137351845

importance of the literal and figurative *place* within which we work, the Academy; for difficult knowledge can, and often does, flourish within the Academy. And yet, the Academy is fraught with privileged modes and ideas of discourse we continue to fight against. Britzman (1998) reminds us that difficult knowledge is important and rightly regarded as wholly human and natural. "To have a human mind" Tuan (2010) notes, "is to live in a world of paradoxes."

Living within a world of paradoxes is difficult. Leaving content aside, the myriad of roles that any one individual takes on is imperative to acknowledge in an academic undertaking. In the case of critically examining K-12 and higher education, tension arises from the fact that we are all at some point or another "teachers" and "learners." Almost everyone can recall an instance of having taught someone some "thing." Similarly, because, at least insofar as the Western world is concerned, schooling is a ubiquitous influence few are exempt from having experienced some form of formal schooling at one point or another.

For our students the paradoxes are even more complex—their views on everything from religion to politics to familial or peer relationships form opaque and diffuse overlays to their core personality and cultural/ environmental upbringing. In addition to reflecting on how we most readily self-identify we consider why writing this with students forced us to examine our own roles and position in the world of education and the Academy. In allowing one another to look critically at each other's writing and ideas a level of classroom intimacy and trust was necessary. When surveying students for this book it came to our attention that the class was split down the middle on some key facets of identity. The class was three quarters women and while we had almost double the number of minority students as a percentage of the class relative to minority enrollment on campus these students readily acknowledged being the "minority voice." Nearly, half of the class identified themselves as consumers of information, people of privilege, and participants in the political process. Only about a third of the students recognized themselves as producers of information or "adults." If we assume that this class of students was more or less representative of the larger university these two particular facts were startling and powerful. They confirmed much of how it could be the case that most students accepted the Forum as it was without any question to the notion of a "banking system of education" as Freire would have called it.

All of the students recognized their role as students and family members that extended to their deep sense/desire of and for community and

DOI: 10.1057/9781137351845

connectedness to others. Some of the most profound notions of identity came from the space on the survey that had an open opportunity for them to comment. One student wanted to be seen and understood as an "advocate" while another wanted to be an impetus for "positive change." Still others made mention of how their previous schooling impacted their ideas. On this note the class was interestingly split between those who had gone to public schools versus private schools as children. Students, as previously noted, were almost universally concerned by their lack of "expertise" and wanted to make clear that diverse disciplinary backgrounds and motivations played into their work. While still a class, writing a collective "book," they also wanted to make their individual identities and approaches apparent; one more paradox in a long, long list for them to make sense of as they wrote and discussed their ideas. Naming and openly acknowledging the paradoxes we worked within allowed that trust to develop over time, and yet a sense of power-laden relationships still clouded our literary endeavor, an important point to punctuate as we move to the student authored chapters. As instructors we issued grades. As students, they issued evaluations. Power and paradox are most certainly present in the tensions seen within the educational solutions presented by our students in the forthcoming chapters, our (we hope) light-handed but directive commentaries, and the incomplete conclusions we draw together about K-12 educational reform.

These paradoxes and the power differential overlaying our endeavor are the last pieces of context, for the writing here is profoundly important. It is why one-size-fits-all solutions do not work at any level of education, it is why one-size-fits-all policies are often short sighted or too narrow, and it is why we knew we must give our students an opportunity to understand their own contexts, our context as a university, and the larger contexts of the K-12 landscape when examining education reform. Power, privilege, and paradox matter to understanding and synthesizing all knowledge. As you read we encourage you to read long enough and deeply enough to see the paradoxes and privilege that they come to terms with in their writing, to feel the justice that students are seeking, to intuit the process which is implied in their solutions, and to acknowledge the thoughtful, disciplined thinking that went into their work. We believe it is a small but powerful treatise on critical discourse and the thinking and learning that follows.

DOI: 10.1057/9781137351845

Notes

1. It's vital to acknowledge the strangeness of the situation of our students who exist in a faux gothic, self-sustained campus with tuition and self-appointed academic restrictions that put attendance out of range for the vast majority of the college eligible population in the United States. That our private university is not representative of the larger collegiate population is vital to note, particularly as we think about what normative assumptions are made and how these function to include or exclude persons who are not, say, "traditional" students of "college age" for example. Suffice to say that if our undergraduates are not considered complete, there are entire swaths of the country that are rendered unintelligible by the frame by which much of education reform is envisioned in the halls of the elite to be foisted onto the schooled halls of the poor.
2. Ideally we would love for the student proposals included in this volume regarding various educational situations as diagnosed both problematic and productive to be viable in the 'real world,' the truth of the matter is that more than anything we wanted them to engage in the process of thinking about and researching through just what reforms and solutions look like when held up to a prism of scrutiny that went beyond sloganeering. It is vital to recall, of course, that this group is in some sense self-selected from courses we have taught in the past and thus, perhaps, their beliefs align with ours in not insignificant ways; however as we had no end in mind for their writing, other than a communal product, our hand is perhaps less heavy than it otherwise might be.
3. For a ready example, note the initial response to a student question at the 1 hour 18 minute mark from the opening Forum event: http://www.youtube.com/watch?v=7BngUH84KVk. In fairness some of the discomfort at such a vital and complex question comes as time is short and panelists have been reminded that they can at best be brief but the reductive responses throughout the short question-and-answer period suggest an unwillingness if not an inability to conceive of students as maintaining their own well informed, complex, and perhaps contrarian notions of educational possibility.
4. For further history on the first Indian Schools see Adams, 1995.
5. For legal precedent of taxation for public education see: *Stuart v School District No. 1 of Village of Kalamazoo*, 30 Mich. 69 (1874).
6. Bain's book, *What the Best College Teachers Do*, was given to all incoming faculty in the College of Arts and Letters at the University of Notre Dame during the academic year 2010–2011 as a welcome gift. Notre Dame has historically placed a great deal of emphasis on teaching and until very recently was thought of predominantly as a undergraduate-based "liberal arts" focused university. In

DOI: 10.1057/9781137351845

recent decades Notre Dame has devoted a great deal of financial resources to building and investing in graduate education and more extensive research platforms and foci University wide. While this is generally seen within the Notre Dame community as a positive investment in the University's future there are some sentiments that this newer focus has come at the expense of the strong, liberal arts-focused reputation of the school.

7 As part of the course and preparation for our writing, students were given an online survey to answer anonymously that allowed us to gather data on the self perceptions of students, their work, and their upbringings.

8 The Henkels lecture series is a competitive grant regularly funded by the Institute for Scholarship in the Liberal Arts at Notre Dame. Two faculty members concerned with the scope (or lack thereof) of the Forum successfully applied for the grant. Speakers included Suzanne Wilson, Gerald Grant, Pauline Lipman, and Kris Gutierrez—all well known and respected educational academicians.

References

Adams, D. W. (1995). *Education for Extinction: American Indians and the Boarding School Experience, 1875–1928*. Lawrence: University Press of Kansas.

Apple, M. (2012). "Foreward". In W. H. Watkins (ed.), *The Assault on Public Education: Confronting the Politics of Corporate School Reform*. New York: Teachers College Press.

Bain, K. (2004). *What the Best College Teachers Do*. Cambridge, Massachusetts: Harvard Press.

Bakhtin, M. (1981). *The Diologic Imagination: Four Essays*. Austin: University of Texas Press.

Bakhtin, M. (1994). *The Bakhtinian Reader: Selected Writings of Bakhtin, Medvedev*. Ed. Voloshinov. London, England: Edward Arnold.

Baudrillard, J. (1994). *Simulacra and Simulation*. Trans. S. F. Glaser. Ann Arbor: University of Michigan Press.

Britzman, D. P. (2003). *Practice Makes Practice: A Critical Study of Learning to Teach*. Albany, New York: State University of New York Press.

Britzman, D. (1998). *Lost Subjects, Contested Objects: Toward a Psychoanalytic Inquiry of Learning*. Albany, New York: State University of New York Press.

Coles, R. (1986). *The Moral Life of Children*. Boston, Massachusetts: Atlantic Monthly Press.

Coles, R. (1990). *The Spiritual Life of Children.* Boston, Massachusetts: Houghton Mifflin Company.
Deegan, M. J. (1988). *Jane Addams and the Men of the Chicago School, 1892–1918.* New Brunswick: Transaction.
Dejoy, N. (2004). *Process This.* Logan: Utah State University Press.
Dewey, J. (1939). *Intelligence in the Modern World: John Dewey's Philosophy.* New York: Modern Library.
Dewey, J. (1902). *The Child and the Curriculum.* Chicago: The University of Chicago Press.
Eisner, E. W. (1994). *The Educational Imagination: On Design and Evaluation of School Programs.* (3rd. ed). New York: Palgrave Macmillan.
Entrada, B. (1994). *Fontana: The Legacy of Spain and Mexico in the United States.* Tucson: Southwest Parks and Monuments Association.
Foucault, M. (1980). *Power/Knowledge: Selected Interviews and Other Writings, 1972–1977.* New York: Pantheon.
Foucault, M. (1972). *The Archaeology of Knowledge.* New York: Vintage Books.
Freire, P. (1974). *Education for Critical Consciousness.* New York: Continuum.
Freud, S. (1949). *The Ego and the Id.* London, England: The Hogarth Press.
Giroux, H. (2012). *Education and the Crisis of Public Values: Challenging the Assault on Teacher, Students, and Public Education.* New York: Peter Lang.
Goffman, E. (1959). *The Presentation of Self in Everyday Life.* New York: Anchor Press.
Katz, M. (1987). *Reconstructing American Education.* Cambridge: Harvard University Press.
Kohlberg, L. (1966). "Moral education in schools: a developmental view". *The School Review.* 74(1), pp. 1–30.
Lonergan, B. (ed.) (1997). *The Lonergan Reader.* Toronto: University of Toronto Press.
Longstreet, W. and Shane, H. G. (1992). *Curriculum for a New Millennium.* New York: Allyn & Bacon.
Notre Dame Forum. (2012). Retrieved February 15, 2012, from http://forum2011.nd.edu/about/
Pennycook, A. (2001). *Critical Applied Linguistics: A Critical Introduction.* Mahwah: Lawrence Erlbaum Associates.
Pinar, W. F. (2001). *The Gender of Racial Politics and Violence in America: Lynching, Prison Rape, & the Crisis of Masculinity* (Vol. 163). New York: Peter Lang.

DOI: 10.1057/9781137351845

Prucha, P. F. (1976). *American Indian Policy in Crisis: Christian Reformers and the Indian, 1864–1900*. Norman: University of Oklahoma Press.
Prucha, P. F. (1984). *The Great Father: The United States Government and the American Indians*. Lincoln: University of Nebraska Press.
Reiss, S. (2004). "Multifaceted nature of intrinsic motivation: the theory of 16 basic desires". *Review of General Psychology*, 8(3), pp. 179–193.
Rorty, R. (1979). *Philosophy and the Mirror of Nature*. Princeton, New Jersey: Princeton University Press.
Rose, M. (1989). *Lives on the Boundary: A Moving Account of the Struggles and Achievements of America's Educationally Underprepared*. New York: Penguin.
Soja, E. W. (1996). *Thirdspace: Journeys to Los Angeles and Other Real-and-Imagined Places*. Cambridge: Blackwell Publishers
Stuart v. school district no. 1 of village of kalamazoo, 30 C.F.R. (1874).
Trites, R. S. (2000). *Disturbing the Universe: Power and Repression in Adolescent Literature*. Iowa City: University of Iowa Press.
Tuan, Y. (1977). *Space and Place: The Perspective of Experience*. Minneapolis, Minnesota: University of Minnesota Press.
Tuan, Y. (2010). "On Paradoxes". Dear Colleague Collection (online collection of Tuan's personal correspondence). Retrieved at: http://www.yifutuan.org/archive/2010/index.htm
Vygotsky, L. (1962/1986). *Thought and Language*. Boston, Massachusetts: MIT Press.
Ward, A. W. (1907). In A. W. Ward and A. R. Waller (eds), *The Cambridge History of English and American Literature*. New York: Putnam. (Reprinted from 2000).
Watkins, W. H. (2012). *The Assault on Public Education: Confronting the Politics of Corporate School Reform*. New York: Teachers College Press.
Williams, J. J. (February 19, 2012). "Deconstructing academe: the birth of critical university studies". *The Chronicle Review*. http://chronicle.com/article/An-Emerging-Field-Deconstructs/130791/
Willinsky, J. (1994). *Empire of Words: The Reign of the OED*. Princeton: Princeton University Press.
Worsham, L. (2002). "Coming to terms: theory, writing, politics". In G. A. Olson (ed.), *Rhetoric and Composition as Intellectual Work* (pp. 101–114). Carbondale: Southern Illinois University Press.

DOI: 10.1057/9781137351845

2
An Editorial Intervention: Mushfaking

Kevin J. Burke, Brian S Collier, and Maria K. McKenna

Abstract: *This brief interlude seeks to frame the subsequent three chapters of student writing, suggesting that the best mode for understanding the student product and processes may be the notion and practice of Mushfake discourse. In this understanding, students came to make do in the clash between their prior schooled lives and the proposal of new models for education rooted in theory beyond their own experiences.*

Collier, Brian S, McKenna, Maria K. and Burke, Kevin J. *College Student Voices on Educational Reform: Challenging and Changing Conversations.* New York: Palgrave Macmillan, 2013. DOI: 10.1057/9781137351845.

Because this book is both about students coming to voice just as it is about student voices responding to the (perceived/invented/real) crisis of school reform in the United States, it becomes important to think through just how this dual consciousness applies in relation to actual student writing for publication. That is, though this is a book de/limited by three academics setting the structural frame of the research through various editorial and stylistic concerns, it is also a text constructed of student writing which will be to degrees both constrained by the experience provided for them through their schooled lives and opened up by the possibility of the public production of knowledge. What we'll propose here is that these three subsequent student chapters from undergraduate students of varying experience and age are, fundamentally and fittingly, a manifestation of what Gee (2001) calls "Mushfake Discourse." Mushfake "means partial acquisition coupled with meta-knowledge and strategies to 'make-do.'" The concept here is borrowed from prison culture where it means "making do with something less when the real thing is not available" (p. 533). The point is not to suggest that our young co-authors here had anything less than a real experience of re-conceptualizing schools; rather we're suggesting that, because this book took form inductively through group work and with precious little traditional guidance from the instructors of the course, they had to, in effect, fake it. The text was not a rhetorical situation for which they'd developed a prior imprint and thus, though they struggled, what they produced rings of earnestness and the honesty of inquiry.

The implications are twofold. Because Gee (p. 526), like Foucault, defines discourses as "ways of being in the world"[1] we can think of the students here, while constructing this text, as constructing new ways to be in the world of school just as they were reflecting on the ways in which school made them. As successful navigators of formal schooling, the students had for the bulk of their lives, for Gee, picked up a "primary Discourse" the "one we first use to make sense of the world and interact with others" (p. 527) regarding the proper modes of literacy instruction, or early childhood education or school environment but also the fundamental formula for being successful in the production of a text for a class. Because Gee does not see primary Discourse as explicitly taught by overt instruction, "but by being a member of a primary socializing group (family, clan, peer group)" (p. 527), it is perhaps fair to say that the primary Discourse of schooling and school literacy for these students was one very much in the mold of most academic

DOI: 10.1057/9781137351845

writing for students: due dates, prescribed parameters for a finished text, and an ultimate output grade over which they have limited control once the text has been submitted, finished and as Jay-Z would say, on to the next one.

Because, however, this is a text that will, in essence, live beyond their time in class and because it was written collaboratively, further because it was written without a prescribed end (we did our best to honor the notion of student voice, by staying out of discussions of what content and conclusions would look like, in hopes that students would engage in the policy conversations we saw as missing in the University Forum), the students outside of their primary school Discourse, were forced to cobble both the writing together, and also the sense of the purpose of the project. They were, in essence, made to mushfake the thing: to invent the problems most pressing in school, and to propose solutions from beyond their own experiences. It was, from the standpoint of the instructor, something of a painful process for the students. They were seeking, again to Gee (2001) here, to pick up a secondary Discourse of school which we "acquire...fluently to the extent that we are given access" to opportunities for practicing it (p. 527). In essence, for Gee, then, these students were picking up literacy, "the mastery of or fluent control over a secondary Discourse" (p. 529) as producers of knowledge that was not proscribed nor prescribed in comfortable and traditional ways, as they wrote the text. Here we have something of what we hope to frame as the "ideological becoming" of our student authors as they went through the very real and painful "process of selectively assimilating the words of others" (Bakhtin, 1981, p. 341). Forced to decide what they believed from the Forum, and forced further to decide what of their experience in schooling counted as at least nominally universal, the student authors made due, mushfaked their way toward a coherent text, and in the end moved beyond the appropriation of authoritative discourse in superficial ways. Rather than choosing to "read and write correctly, and complete tasks dutifully...without being genuinely engaged either with the ideas or the process" (Landay, 2004, p. 113) the students turned a course on educational policy into a "writing class...the site at which students and teachers produce literacy" (Penticoff and Brodkey, 1996, p. 244). The work of this book as a whole is in helping students "position themselves intellectually to acquire agency in their worlds" (Olson, 2002, p. 84). There are a number of implications to this approach, but primary for our concerns here is the sense of making do.

DOI: 10.1057/9781137351845

If we return to the origin of the term, then we find that in prison culture, something that is mushfaked is often viewed as contraband. Certainly we might explore further the somewhat strange, though sadly increasingly correlated, links between prison and schooling, but the most pressing issue to note before we turn finally to student text is this idea that something has been fashioned, in secret, from re-purposed materials for the sake of function. We can't speak on how this text will come to function beyond its publishing, but we're certain that from our perspective as teachers and editors and theorists (mushfakers all) the value has been in the whittling, the arguing, the clandestiness, all of which tends to go out the window with a polished and finished product. It's our hope that the becoming of expertise and the, even if tentative, agency of being expert in something colors the discourse of these next chapters.

References

Bakhtin, M. M. (1981). "Discourse and the novel". In M. Holquist (ed.), *The Dialogic Imagination: Four Essays by M. M. Bakhtin.* Trans. Caryl Emerson and Michael Holquist. Austin: University of Texas Press.

Gee, J. P. (2001). "Literacy, discourse, and linguistics: introduction". In E. Cushman, E. Kintgen, B. Kroll and M. Rose (eds), *Literacy: A Critical Sourcebook.* New York: Bedford/St. Martin's.

Landay, E. (2004). "Performance as the foundation for a secondary school literacy program: a Bakhtinian perspective". In A. F. Ball and S. W. Freedman (eds), *Bakhtinian Perspectives on Language, Literacy, and Learning* (pp. 107–128). New York: Cambridge University Press.

Olson, G. A. (ed.) (2002). *Rhetoric and Composition as Intellectual Work.* Carbondale: Southern Illinois University Press.

Penticoff, R. and Brodkey, L. (1996). "Writing about difference: 'hard cases' for cultural studies". In L. Brodkey (ed.), *Writing Permitted in Designated Areas Only* (pp. 228–245). Minneapolis: University of Minnesota Press.

DOI: 10.1057/9781137351845

3

Literacy: Fostering Lifelong Learning

David Berton Grau, Kathleen B. Mullins, and Katherine A. Puszka with Kevin J. Burke

Abstract: *This chapter, as conceptualized by the three student authors, frames early literacy as of primary importance in fostering success in schooling. This is not surprising, of course, given the extensive corpus that yet grows on the topic; unique here, however, is the work that Grau, Mullins and Puszka do in disentangling, through narrative intervals, their own successful schooled experiences from larger proposals for educational policy change. That is, the authors use the experience of their schooling to suggest, but not prescribe, ways forward for fostering long-term success for all students in American K-12 education in the realm of literacy.*

Collier, Brian S, McKenna, Maria K. and Burke, Kevin J. *College Student Voices on Educational Reform: Challenging and Changing Conversations*. New York: Palgrave Macmillan, 2013. DOI: 10.1057/9781137351845.

Foreword

What follows is a student-authored chapter. Necessarily the text is limited, as is all text, by the experiences and discourses with which these authors have experience. Because these are undergraduate students, minoring (or having minored) in education, their exposure to various theories and histories about the production of, in particular, literacy and literacy instruction in schools is patently limited. This does not mean, however, that they are devoid of a special knowledge, nor is this foreword meant to undermine the very real and thoughtful work the students have done going forward. Rather what we seek to do here is provide some broader context, a bit of theoretical grounding for the conclusions drawn while also drawing attention to a proposal for a twofold mode of reading of the student text as written.

Reading

Brian Huot (2002) argues that "teachers need to realize that all of our experiences with students, classrooms, curricula and institutions have the ability to affect the way we read student writing" (p. 121). We would agree. Particularly because student writing in academic texts is primarily situated as problematic or perhaps illustrative of the mechanics of writing itself for the sake of teaching skills, we would suggest that there is precious little precedent for reading student writing in the mode of ideological becoming, as possessive of intent and true force. While it's certainly true that these students have not legislated educational policy, nor have they taught in the traditional sense—nor have a great number of the people billed as experts in the public sphere these days; it seems that experience in education as in government is more cause for vilification at present, but that's another issue for another time—they are still, we think, producers of knowledge that can become valuable in the execution of the improvement of schools and in this chapter's sense, the approach to the teaching of literacy in education writ large. We would note the inherent danger of lionizing the kinds of conclusions that come out of the beknighted naiveté of Lortie's (1975) "apprenticeship of observation" but suggest that the students here, particularly in the structural organization of the chapter, begin with their own histories in literacy education not to mythologize, but rather to point toward areas for further study.

DOI: 10.1057/9781137351845

With that in mind, we'd suggest that a reader approach the foregoing text with something like a dual vision. First, it makes sense of course to read for the implicit and explicit policy implications for K-12 education as suggested by the student text. There are novel ideas and there are restatements of current educational successes as well as cautions regarding problematic and thorny roads education has already taken. As any good writer, the students find gaps in practice and theory, exploit them, and work at the edges of the possible in their prose drawing extensively on their own experiences and on the work of others in the field. This is, of course, good news. Second, however, we would suggest reading the text for the implications of the collaborative work of students' ideological becoming. Through the semester and year, students were tasked with constructing an ethos, a theme, articulating a problem, pursuing it and then molding a textual argument for an unknown audience (you). The complexity of the rhetorical situation was such that, well, the professors in the course never quite elucidated what a solution to an existent problem might look like. And so the students began without prescribed readings and had to pursue their own hunches, collaboratively. They were nascent researchers and so should be read as such, not sympathetically we think, but empathetically with a view toward the possible in student writing when the end product is not a grade or a term paper, but rather a solution to a problem in the world. This is high-minded rhetoric, we realize, but it's worth wondering what's wrong with that as we dive in.

Introduction

For children, literacy opens the floodgates to a boundless supply of knowledge, providing the means for insight into any topic imaginable and the method to experience the world in new ways. In a country where the written word pervades nearly every facet of society, literacy is arguably the most crucial building block for achievement throughout all levels of education and in the workforce. Yet far too many children lack proficient literacy skills. According to results from the National Assessment of Educational Progress (NAEP) reading test in 2009, 68% of fourth grade public school students in the US failed to reach the "proficient" level in reading; of children from low-income families, 83% failed to reach proficiency (National Center for Education Statistics, 2009). Leaving aside our own general skepticism of large-scale standardized testing, as a broad measure, these numbers are unacceptable. In order to create a strong future foundation, students must be able to sufficiently read, write, and analyze. However, in a society run through with competition for increasingly complex jobs "proficiency" is obviously no longer adequate. As such, educators must strive to re-think the system and re-structure literacy education so that it is able to spark, maintain, and continually encourage individual interest, even into adult life. Only in this way, where educational progress and achievement transcend the limiting confines of high-stakes testing and complement personal interest and growth, will students ever be able to truly develop as literate individuals.

This chapter, then, is our attempt to outline challenges that exist in preparing students for competency in literacy in schools. To do this we engage personal narratives to illustrate what success might look like from the standpoint of nascent researchers, while linking to some significant current theory to add heft to our argument.

Confronting the challenge: elevating literacy today

With the contemporary culture of education so intensely focused on issues like accountability, standardized testing, and the evaluation of students, teachers, and schools, literacy instruction and student knowledge have suffered, leading to myopic attempts at reform. Instead of focusing on creating lifelong readers in a holistic way, our schools, districts, states, and federal government have locked-in on improving the literacy assessment numbers that result from what is often a single battery of tests within a given year. Given the larger climate of education, this is logical, as these tests and their results greatly influence decisions regarding student placement, teacher tenure and salary, the retention of principals and superintendents, and the election prospects of politicians. Indeed the tests have come to outline the very survival of individual schools. We feel this is not, however, an ideal or even passable environment for fostering students' passions for reading and addressing the individualized needs of our students.

The contemporary environment of education is in large part the result of the federal government's requirements—most notably in No Child Left Behind (NCLB) and increasingly the Race to the Top—that states must test their students and complete certain types of analyses with the

DOI: 10.1057/9781137351845

resultant data. While most states utilized standardized testing before the enactment of NCLB, this landmark piece of legislation mandated universal testing and began tying various punishments to poor tests results, thus pushing our nation toward the "accountability" rhetoric so prevalent today. Just as significantly, NCLB also allowed each state to determine their own definition of "proficiency" for their students and examinations. As a result, a majority of states now have vague or even borderline meaningless standards, dumbed down to allow more students to pass examinations[1] (Ravitch, 2010). In "The Test Mess," Traub (2002) sums up the peculiar lunacy of these high-stakes examinations in the schools of the United States: "The whole episode is a painful proof of the absurdity of thinking that testing, all by itself, will raise the academic performance of children who have muddled along in school for years" (p. 351). Taking what are essentially outcome variables (student achievement on standardized tests), highly dependent on forces (poverty, for instance) beyond schools, and grafting them onto an explanation for teacher efficacy belies the complex nature of society and does a disservice to schooling as a whole. Moreover, this thinking does not apply only to students, but to teachers, administrators, schools, districts, and states as well. Thus, all of these groups are directly linked to the consequences of standardized testing as a result of the new emphasis on accountability.

Due to the importance of testing and the burgeoning culture of accountability, many district decisions and specific actions by teachers are motivated by the considerations of testing. States and districts strive to improve their tests scores, yet attempt to do so on tests that are constantly being re-centered around the average. We might ask, as did "Wendy Darling"[2] (2002), "How can 90% of our students read at grade level as measured by our norm-referenced test, which was constructed so that 50% of the test-takers will score below grade level (whatever that is)"(p. 314). These test scores are further complicated by research arguing that approximately 50 to 80 % of standardized test scores can be attributed to random influences, rather than demonstrating a clear correlation with student knowledge and ability ("Darling," 2002). As states and schools strive to "raise standards" and improve student, teacher, and school performance, they are stuck with the utter absurdity of the situation. How can we truly raise test scores using an evaluation that is crafted to ensure that half of the students still remain "below" the threshold for competency? Standards and learning objectives are not moving targets, but should be firmly rooted based on our goals for students' knowledge

DOI: 10.1057/9781137351845

by grade level. Students who can perform and meet the level of these objectives on an evaluation should be positively acknowledged for this achievement instead of compared to the overall performance of peers in their age group. Education, in other words, might better be conceived as measured by individual progress rather than as aggregate gains placed against the backdrop of a need to account for a mythologized normal curve of learning. But that's a larger discussion for another day; for now, back to the states.

With their ability to set their own standards, many states and test-makers across the country are ratcheting down the difficulty of exit exams as a means to claim improved results. In order to be effective, tests should accurately measure student performance and knowledge based on a given set of objectives. In lowering the standards of our state and national tests, we are accepting a level of performance that does not actually meet the benchmarks originally laid out for our students. As a result, students are able to graduate high school with the requisite grades to enroll in college, yet they ultimately arrive to those college campuses in need of remedial instruction. Conversely, many other industrialized nations put their students through far more rigorous academic programs than those typical in the United States (Traub, 2002). Instead of our highly decentralized system of education, these nations have either a prescribed national curriculum or highly specific national standards, with end-of-the-year exams to test whether students have mastered the prescribed material. Although the doctrine of local school control may be too highly valued and established in the United States to allow for such rigorous national standards, states must—at the very least—hold themselves to high standards. Whether the Common Core movement achieves this remains to be seen. At any rate, the aim should be to improve students' knowledge and abilities, rather than simply increase the number of "proficient" test takers.

In this rush to improve standardized test scores, curricula are often tailored specifically to the areas evaluated by testing, thus failing to provide students with the full breadth of academic and cultural exposure they should be receiving. It is this narrowing of the curriculum to mirror the questions of last year's test and the biases inherent in high-stakes testing that most forcefully impacts the schooling experiences of America's most disadvantaged students.

We might think about how this affects very specific cultural biases and reads them onto schools. For example, a student may choose to write

DOI: 10.1057/9781137351845

an essay on one of Langston Hughes's many poems that feature African American Vernacular English, but he is required to write it in what the test-makers deem to be "Standard English" or else his score will suffer dramatically. Ignored are the complexities that might lead a student to mirror the linguistic decisions of an author in order to more fully engage an analysis. But such are the losses when one is batch processing test scores for ease of assessment rather than for what we might call genuine learning in certain environs. As an even greater irony, in order for that student to perform well on the English Language Arts portion of that test, his class's curriculum is often narrowed to such a point that there is no longer time for the works of Langston Hughes or the countless other authors and poets who wrote in the vernacular form of language that may appeal to various students.

In spite of its problematic nature, however, high-stakes testing is certainly not purposely intended to narrow and limit classroom curricula; rather, its national implementation was originally intended to provide schools and educators with high quality, richly detailed data about students, teachers, and schools. This information was then meant to function as the impetus and source of direction for improvements to the system. As "Darling" (2002) notes, "The politicians say that we are giving these tests in order to learn something about achievement. That is, these numbers are supposed to tell teachers something that we can use for the purpose of teaching better" (p. 315). And yet in reality, high-stakes standardized testing does not ultimately benefit the feedback and instruction process; instead, it places teachers under the pressing weight of accountability and forces them to focus solely on test preparation and subsequently resort to repeatedly drilling their students on concentrated subject material. In this way, standardized testing is flawed by design, and it fails to fulfill its intended purpose of providing the necessary data to improve schools. Instead, it has created a feedback loop in which test preparation has negatively invaded and diluted the curriculum. As a result, standardized testing accurately reflects students' abilities to cram for the tests themselves, yet it fails to provide any meaningful analysis of students' knowledge of the full scope of the literacy curriculum.

Existing within an educational environment that continuously emphasizes accountability and values pure statistics, high-stakes standardized testing will persist into the foreseeable future spinning into ever more profitable ends for the Pearsons of the world at the expense of,

DOI: 10.1057/9781137351845

well, perhaps our students' capacities to formulate arguments, to write complexly, to argue vehemently. Instead, we feel, the system must be re-imagined and re-constituted in such a way that it more accurately reflects students' abilities, encompasses the full breadth of the literacy curriculum, and improves teacher instruction and student learning. Toward this end, standardized testing should evolve from its current state into a system of diagnostic testing. Such tests would allow teachers and educators to better understand the areas in which students require remediation and would act as useful tools, rather than dreaded high-stakes evaluations. In order to improve the value of standardized testing as a diagnostic tool for teachers and an evaluative measure for school leaders and policymakers, tests also need to be taken at more frequent intervals throughout the year. By documenting student ability and comprehension at multiple points, teachers and policymakers would both have a more accurate understanding of the development of their students and be better positioned to improve their own actions and foster future learning.

Despite the potential benefits of standardized testing as a diagnostic tool, the present environment of education ultimately presents a challenge to our vision of a holistic, interest-based system of literacy instruction and development. With such an intense emphasis on skill instruction and test results, the need to engage students and develop their passion for reading is far too often overlooked. Only, we think, with a strong focus on students' interests and passion for reading, will our children develop as literate citizens who excel in the classroom and beyond. Tests are one measure of aptitude; we'd suggest looking to others for the sake of students and their future roles as leaders, writers, readers and citizens.

Sparking the flame of curiosity

The ultimate byproduct of standardized testing is that children very quickly lose interest in school. As lack of interest leads to lack of effort which leads to poor performance, it is of necessary importance to focus on finding a way to spark interest in every child. Only through interest and curiosity can students make the transition from *learning to read* to *reading to learn*. Yet "reading to learn" presents a challenge in an age where the purpose of learning has been narrowed so excessively by

DOI: 10.1057/9781137351845

accountability regimes. If students come to believe that the purpose of learning is to perform well on a test, then so too will they come to believe that reading shares this purpose. This toxic way of thinking has poisoned many classrooms, and it presents a monumental obstacle to fostering a literate, inquisitive generation of kids. In order to help students adopt the idea of "reading to learn" in the proper sense, educators need (the freedom within their positions) to encourage students to re-think the purpose of learning, to view it not as performing well on tests but rather as acquiring knowledge, one of life's greatest joys. Students need to really believe that learning is *fun*, for finding enjoyment in learning encourages a posture of curiosity and excitement. Curiosity is pivotal in the classroom as it encourages the development of an active mind and makes a student keen and observant of new ideas. Furthermore, it illuminates new worlds of possibilities and brings excitement to learning. Teachers must spark student curiosity in learning before any real progress can be achieved. In order to ultimately re-shape students' ideology, teachers should be examples of lifelong learners; infuse the classroom with energy, passion, and creativity; recognize students' work; and above all, know, love, and believe in their students, regardless of race, class, discipline problems, or academic success.

In order to propel a student to value learning and develop a thirst for knowledge, teachers must personally exemplify and embody the idea of curious, lifelong learners. Ron Clark, a middle school teacher and co-founder of the Ron Clark Academy, a private non-profit school in Atlanta, Georgia, emphasizes this point in his most recent book, *The End of Molasses Classes: Getting Our Kids Unstuck—101 Extraordinary Solutions for Parents and Teachers*. Criticizing teachers that lie when asked questions to which they do not know the answer so as to appear all-knowing, Clark (2011) explains that "the real lesson we need to teach our children is that the man (sic) who can actually find the answers to any question presented to him is the true genius" (p. 58). Teachers should be bouncing off the walls with eagerness in an attempt to infect students with the desire to seek knowledge and to demonstrate the joy they themselves receive from learning new things. This is especially essential in middle school and high school, when subject material starts to become more theoretically complex. Engaging students who are struggling with reading will be an immense challenge for teachers if these students do not first have a desire to unveil what knowledge the reading withholds.

DOI: 10.1057/9781137351845

Telling stories

Teachers who foster this element of questioning and discovery within children are the most influential and memorable teachers, and it is with them that children can develop a lifelong passion for learning.

Recalling my own education,[3] *one teacher stands out as a true representative of a lifelong learner whose classroom enthusiasm was simply contagious and propelled me to actively participate every day. Mr. Wilson*[4] *taught Advanced Placement (AP) European History, a class that covers over six hundred years of content. This class and its required reading could have been exceedingly boring and irrelevant to everyday life had Mr. Wilson not been so enthusiastic about the subject himself. He constantly made connections between current events and history, oftentimes bringing in articles he found that somehow tied into the day's lesson. Though he was infectiously animated everyday, Mr. Wilson's enthusiasm is most exemplified in the way in which he handled the actual day of the AP test, a stressful and nerve-racking day for many students. While most AP teachers on test-day might attempt to calm their students' nerves by offering a reassuring "Good luck!" before sending them into the designated test-taking room, Mr. Wilson organized a send-off that completely destroyed the stale, intense atmosphere of testing and erased any and all nerves we might have had. He began the send-off by gathering us all in his room and having our high school football coach give us an intense, fiery pep talk, one that made it feel as if we were about to run onto a field to win the biggest game of the season, not into a large lecture hall to complete the toughest test of the year. Then, in an attempt to mimic the "storming of the Bastile," a markéd moment in France's history, Mr. Wilson had us literally storm the halls of our high school. As French revolutionary music blasted from someone's iHome, we ran cheering and screaming through the entirety of the high school, following Mr. Wilson's lead, before charging the testing room itself. Much to the surprise of the slightly startled test chaperone, we burst into the room in high spirits—laughing, panting, and pumping with adrenaline. We were ready to take on the world, and the AP test suddenly seemed manageable and accessible.*

By truly adopting the identity of a passionate, dynamic lifelong learner, Mr. Wilson made his students realize the potential for European history to be not only accessible but interesting and exciting. Creating this exciting environment was crucial, for it instilled in me a curiosity to learn more about the subject matter, which in turn propelled me to actually read and engage myself in the text. Had I not been invested in the class, I would not have been nearly as motivated to complete the readings. The fact that this example refers to senior

DOI: 10.1057/9781137351845

year in high school sheds light on the necessity for sparking interest in students of all ages, across all grades. Literacy is not a one-step process; it is a faculty that demands consistent nurturing throughout one's life. In order to both instill and sustain a love of reading in students, teachers need to constantly evoke in them curiosity and excitement, two qualities that can propel them to seek and desire knowledge and to uphold literature as the gateway to do so.

Sparking a lifelong passion for literature

While curiosity is the incendiary agent that can catalyze a student's love for learning, it is also important to initiate and maintain student interest in reading and writing. Educators must not discount the immeasurable value of personalized and individualized student attention in these areas; once a child is interested in reading and writing, continued personal attention from an adult can reinforce and foster this interest. If curiosity is the initial spark that ignites interest in education, then individualized attention is the necessary fuel that will sustain further growth.

From personal experience,[5] *I have recognized that this special attention can truly make the difference between literary appreciation and understanding versus utter frustration and disillusionment. For example, when I was in the first grade, I was disinterested in reading, and my achievement suffered as a result. Thankfully, I had a passionate teacher who was committed to helping her students develop a love for reading. Cognizant of my struggles, she enrolled me in an additional reading program where I worked with the school's literacy specialist and a few other students in small-scale exercises that afforded each of us extra attention in the specific areas we were lacking. When I returned to regular classes after working in this program for most of my first grade year, my teacher immediately detected my newfound interest in reading. Over the years, this interest grew into a passion, and by the third and fourth grades I was already devouring books at a rate that many of my classmates found unusual. This passion grew into a hunger for learning and new texts, and by the time I was in high school I knew that I wanted to pursue a career path that complemented my love for literature. Now I am an undergraduate English major, and more than ever I appreciate the immense value of reading and writing. These are lifelong skills that aid success, despite a person's job title. If one develops an affinity for reading, then a surprising amount of doors will be open in the future.*

Furthermore, not only does reading increase vocabulary skills, but it also unlocks imagination and allows people to view the world in ways they may not

DOI: 10.1057/9781137351845

have formerly thought possible. This passion for reading is most significant when fostered and developed at an early age. Good teachers, literacy programs, and parental support can truly help create the foundation upon which students can build a lifelong love of learning. For example, the special attention I was given dramatically improved my life. If my disinterest and remedial literacy skills had been initially ignored, I would have undoubtedly been ushered into an unbroken cyclical system of increasingly low literacy achievement. Basic literacy skills are not often taught after the primary grades because students are expected to have already formed a strong background and ability to read. However, if these skills are not initially cultivated, they will most likely not be addressed in subsequent grades, when the focus shifts from learning to read to reading to learn. If a student does not learn to read correctly, then he or she will never be able to live up to his or her full potential to learn. Thus, students who are struggling in the primary grades must be given special attention and placed into additional literacy programs to bolster their reading confidence and ability.

In addition to my education as a primary student, my more recent experiences as a young adult interested in education have only reaffirmed my more youthful conviction that it is necessary and critical to provide students with individualized attention when teaching and developing literacy skills. Through my personal observations participating in teaching and tutoring programs, I have experienced the inherent value of personalized attention. For example, last fall I participated in the Appalachia Seminar through the Center for Social Concerns at the University of Notre Dame. This program teaches college students about the lifestyles and social preoccupations of the people of the Appalachian region and includes a one-week immersion to a particular site in the region, during which students assist with a myriad of activities ranging from home construction to neighborhood restoration to education. My particular site was a small high school in David, Kentucky, and my group and I spent the week shadowing and tutoring thirty students. Notre Dame tutors participated in different activities as per their specific talents and creative niches, and, as an English major, I was assigned to work primarily with students in English class.

Although it may not be fully recognized as a controversial topic in modern society, illiteracy is a pervasive problem in the United States, particularly in the Appalachian region. The students that I worked with at the David School, for example, were in high school, but their reading and comprehension abilities were significantly below projected grade level skill. Thus, it was quite challenging for me to adjust my methods of teaching study skills and tweak them in a way so that they would pertain to students who performed below average. Frustratingly, I found that many of the students quickly dismissed the value of

DOI: 10.1057/9781137351845

reading and a culture of literacy in general, and this acknowledged refusal to learn and participate severely cut them off from achieving any real progress. Reading was perceived as "uncool," and thus some students refused to participate in class activities so as to preserve their social status. In addition to skill level, this social barrier made it even more difficult for me to attain credibility and respect among these students.

I found, however, that over the course of the week I began to establish good peer relationships with the students that made it significantly easier for us to work together. Because I was close to these students in age, I believe that they felt they could more easily relate to me than they could their traditional teacher, and thus they were more receptive to the information I shared with them. I also strived to make reading fun and relatable to the students as individuals, and this helped them reconsider their perspectives towards certain facets of reading and writing. For example, throughout the week I concentrated my time tutoring two boys, Chris and Jack,[6] *in reading and writing. During one class period they were assigned to convert their lists of contrasting descriptions into paragraphs about an ocean versus a lake. They were a little resistant, but I kept encouraging them, and once they got going they didn't seem to mind the work too much. I noticed Chris had copied a whole sentence from the story into his own assignment, so I told him about plagiarism, quotation marks, and citing sources. I knew this was a great deal of information to absorb, so I tried to break it up into manageable components and keep it relatively simple. I think he came to grasp the concept, so I made him repeat what I had just explained. He was initially unsure how to react, but I saw him responding to my personalized attention, and the wheels of thought began to move.*

I also tried to help them recognize that writing should sound different than speaking. At first, Chris was offended because he thought I was criticizing the "unintelligent" way he spoke with his regional accent, but then I explained how this difference applies to everyone, not just people from Appalachia. I used the example of text messages, novels, and everyday speech, and described that while all these were forms of communication, they are inherently different in style and approach; just like a text message has a different composition than a novel, so must his class writing have a different style than his normal, colloquial speech. Chris understood this analogy immediately, and it helped him recognize that literary conventions are universal (though of course culturally situated) and are not derived in an effort to personally confuse him.

Ultimately, with one-on-one peer tutoring, these high school boys from rural Kentucky were able to recognize an entry point of personal interest within the literature they were studying that subsequently helped engage them with the

DOI: 10.1057/9781137351845

rest of the material. Given my, admittedly limited, experience I believe it is important to approach literacy on a per pupil basis and treat each student as an individual. Furthermore, teachers must challenge students while still explaining concepts to them in ways that they can more concretely understand. Even if it is done in marginal ways, by curtailing lesson plans to consider the strengths, weaknesses, and interests of individuals, educators will be better able to spark and maintain student interest and potentially spur a lifelong appreciation for reading. Systemic reform may be needed, and much change will need to take place in order for students to truly be able to achieve significant literacy improvement, however teachers can implement small changes in order to work towards this greater goal. Even a brief daily exchange and check-in with students as they are working on in-class assignments can allow educators insight into students' interests so that they can provide them with valuable insight and direction. Thus, teachers should strive to achieve the progress they can, even on small levels, and fight against the system from within by providing individualized attention within their current education environments.

Making literature come alive: extracurricular activities

Once educators ignite curiosity and maintain student interest through specialized attention, they can continue to cultivate and foster improvement in literacy by adapting reading, writing, and storytelling to other creative outlets that make literature come to life. This additional element allows students to relate to what they learn inside the classroom and then go one step further and apply those lessons to their everyday lives. If done correctly, these useful skills can transcend a child's formative education years and continue to enhance their life into adulthood.

One way in which educators can add an extra dimension to literature and create a compelling literary environment is by taking occasional classroom trips to the school or public library. Additionally, teachers can create accessible, in-class libraries and encourage students to return and check books out. In any capacity, libraries provide an excellent atmosphere in which students can surround themselves with books and other people who *enjoy* reading. Furthermore, librarians can act as aides to teachers, helping students individually select books or magazines that adhere to their specific interests. This individualization and special attention helps directly apply literature to students' lives and engages them in materials that are personally stimulating and pertinent.

DOI: 10.1057/9781137351845

We acknowledge the privileged position from which we write these things. Many schools, particularly those in inner-cities and especially recently created for-profit and online charter schools simply don't have libraries. This can be attributed to a great many factors, but we might easily tie the lamentable situation to penalties tied to funding that have been prevalent since the passage of NCLB. That teachers must draw from their own funds to provide meager libraries for kids is no new phenomenon, but that they are the only books in the school comes to remind us of the conditions of Jim Crow schools prior to *Brown*. This is, perhaps, not surprising considering the large-scale re-segregation of public schooling in the last 30-odd years (Kozol, 2005).

There is significant merit in *choice* and personal interest when it comes to reading, and often students rebel against texts that teachers assign, viewing them as boring and inapplicable to contemporary issues. Unfortunately, this sentiment keeps many students from allowing the texts enough time to prove otherwise. However, if students were allowed to read what they *want* to read, perhaps this would provide a broader appreciation for literature and establish a comfort zone and resulting level of confidence that would allow them to explore other texts in the classroom. What students need is that one book that will hook them on reading for life; once a student experiences the struggles and joys of grappling with a challenging text that pertains to their interests, it becomes significantly more plausible that they can similarly master other texts. Libraries allow the ideal environment in which this initial catalyst can foster that confidence. As aforementioned, it is important for teachers to provide individualized attention within the classroom, but if more resources reinforce this sentiment, the more a passion for reading and writing will likely grow and resonate within children. Indeed, as Esquith (2007) describes:

> We are trying to establish a set of values in our children; it helps when they are surrounded by others who share a fervor for reading. At the library, children can browse and make discoveries that wouldn't be possible online; at the same time they can interact with readers of all ages instead of just opening a package that shows up in their mailbox. (p. 38)

This additional exposure is advantageous from an intellectual perspective, but it also reinforces the idea that reading is not "nerdy," but fun. Our society is one of constant entertainment and instant gratification, and many times reading becomes a passive, uninteresting pastime that

DOI: 10.1057/9781137351845

has negative connotations among students because it is not as thrilling or stimulating as other activities. Parent and teacher support, however, helps fortify the notion that reading is a valuable and meaningful pursuit. Thus, educators should organize regular class trips to libraries in order to spur the development of enjoyment, passion, and culture for reading.

Another way to create stimulating and effective reading environments is to create learning-based extracurricular activities such as school book clubs or competitive reading teams. Given the pervasive influence of standardized testing and strict district requirements for specific lesson plans, curriculum is often limited or curtailed in a way that does not provide students with an individualized, stimulating literary environment. Often *fun* is substituted for *standards*, and while standards must necessarily exist, educators should not completely eliminate student enjoyment from their lesson plans. One way that teachers can compensate for this stimulation is by creating book clubs or competitive reading programs during student lunch periods or after school hours. In this way, reading becomes a group activity and helps eliminate one of the common misconceptions that young people have today, "that reading is something we study only during English class" (Esquith, 2007, p. 40). Reading is a lifelong, necessary skill, and the more that students engage in it outside of traditional classroom contexts, the more they will hone their skills and enhance their vocabulary. Additionally, these extracurricular literary programs help convey to children that reading is an enjoyable, mainstream activity as opposed to a stigmatized "nerdy" one. Indeed, in this context:

> the students participate voluntarily, so the teacher is working with enthusiastic young people. The kids get to meet like-minded peers from other classes whom they might not have gotten to know otherwise. Friendships are formed. The teacher bonds with young scholars in a different environment, which strengthens the teacher-student relationship in the classroom. (p. 7)

Essentially the stage is set: children are provided an interesting social environment in which to potentially help foster their future love of reading.

I personally found this type of program rewarding as a result of my own experiences as a middle school student.[7] *For example, in the third and fourth grades I was part of a literacy program called "Battle of the Books," where students formed teams of four or five and met weekly to compete in a contest*

DOI: 10.1057/9781137351845

that consisted of questions from about fifteen staff-approved, award-winning books. This program was surprisingly competitive, and it culminated in a championship round with trophies at the end of the year. Parents and friends came to the event and helped create a very supportive, educationally charged environment. The program encouraged all of the student participants to read the listed texts and answer questions for points, but it also spurred us to discuss texts outside of battles in order to check our understanding and thus improve our winning odds. Programs like this are extremely effective in spurring interest and passion for reading because they create an atmosphere where reading is encouraged and celebrated, and they also hold students accountable for a number of additional, outside novels that they read as a result of their own initiative.

In addition to extracurricular activities that are specifically centered around traditional veins of literacy such as reading and writing, there is great merit and value to a student developing greater creative and analytical skills through unorthodox, hands-on avenues, such as theater. Teachers must aim to be innovative and incorporate creativity into the classroom, and one of the best ways to get a student excited about reading, especially a struggling student, is to make reading transcend the page on stage. As a theater major and musician,[8] *I am an advocate for the arts and especially for their presence in schools. I have witnessed firsthand the influence the arts can have on a child's life, particularly through the experience of my close friend and cousin, Jack, who shares my love for theater and the arts. Our treasured experience of childhood was participating in a local children's theater that provided the opportunity for children in grades three through eight to participate in two productions each year. These productions were entirely formative in both of our lives, giving us an outlet to grow, to create, to imagine, to play, and to think outside the box. Moreover, they contributed in a particular way to the enhancement of Jack's reading skills. Though Jack loved performing, he did not enjoy reading, particularly cold reading, a term used by actors to refer to reading aloud from a script or other text without any rehearsal, practice or study in advance. On the first day of rehearsal, then, when we received our scripts and proceeded to read our parts aloud for the first time, Jack often stumbled and took a longer time to get through the text. In concentrating solely on reading the words, he generally failed to speak the lines with the right inflection and to convey their meaning. Essentially, sitting and reading the words tied him down and restrained him from being able to access the text. Only as we continued through the rehearsal process and Jack began memorizing his lines did a dramatic transformation occur. Once free from the page, he was able to explore character development,*

DOI: 10.1057/9781137351845

delve into the intricacies of the plot, and bring the story to life in a way he never could in the classroom.

This method of transcending the page was in fact so effective that Jack transferred to a school particularly tailored to the visual and performing arts, a place where his learning would not be limited by traditional classroom methods. In positioning the arts at the heart of every classroom, the school allowed Jack to creatively engage with texts every day, and he soon became increasingly proficient at reading. He always understood the text best when it was taught in a way that brought it to life, when he could adopt the identity of different characters and explore in a real way their motives, actions, and personalities. Theater strongly impacted his ability to analyze, to think critically, and to apply what he was learning to other aspects of his life. Appropriately, Jack ended up studying musical theater at The Boston Conservatory before making his way successfully to the Great White Way.

Clearly, Jack is an exceptional case. Yet there is immense potential for growth in all children through the integration of arts in the classroom, even in small ways. According to Allington (2008) "In most schools struggling readers are lucky if they spend 10 to 20 percent of their school day in lessons designed to meet their needs" (p. 2). Instead, these children endure long days during which engagement in class activities is difficult and long nights during which homework is arduous. Without individual attention paid to these students, the possibility of them falling through the cracks becomes almost imminent. Through the incorporation of creativity in the classroom, these suffering students may be able to view reading as fun and engaging, as opportunity to explore new people and places. Schools and afterschool programs alike need to capitalize on this opportunity to engage students and to reach them in ways traditional teaching styles may fail. If students can first fall in love with storytelling, they can then fall in love with engagement with the texts of the stories themselves. As Clark (2011) notes, "There is always a way to bring learning to life and to place eagerness in the hearts of our children, and we owe it to them to find it" (p. 84). Through a renewed focus on curriculum and a dedication to the cultivation of curiosity, excitement, and creativity in each individual student, educators may be able to dramatically improve the state of literacy in our schools.

Conclusion

Ultimately, educators must develop and implement strategies that foster literate practice among their students. This is, we think, different from

DOI: 10.1057/9781137351845

the drill and kill approach to grammar and vocabulary. In a 21st century society, students must be able to apply literature to their lives in order to spark stimulation and encourage continued interest in reading. If students read for pleasure and are able to derive personal meaning from the texts that they study, they will be more likely to continue building upon this interest and skill in their educational lives and excel academically. Esquith (2007) suggests that, "Young people who read for pleasure are able to make connections with the world around them and eventually grow to understand themselves on levels they never thought possible" (p. 43). Through this process of reading and self-discovery, students make the connections between text and their own experiences that foster their passion for reading and ultimately lead to academic improvement overall. Reading those texts mandated by the state in preparation for their standardized tests may not yield these significant improvements in achievement; only a love for reading and an interest in learning will provide meaningful gains in literacy attainment, measurable or otherwise. A passion for reading is an immeasurable gift that, if approached in the right way, can help stimulate students for the rest of their lives. If you give a student a book, she reads for a day; if you teach a student the passions of reading, then she learns for a lifetime. Only through fostering this love of reading in our nation's students will they ultimately thrive in the classroom and develop the necessary skills to help build the future.

Notes

1 It remains to be seen what the effects of the movement toward the Common Core State Standards will have at the classroom level, though we are not particularly sunny on the prospects that testing will be deemphasized nor that student difficulties will be wiped away by a new round of aspirational targets.
2 The author – "Wendy Darling" – chose to use a pseudonym.
3 The following is a personal anecdote by one of the authors.
4 For the privacy of the individual, Mr. Wilson is a pseudonym.
5 The following is a personal anecdote by one of the authors.
6 For the privacy of the individuals, Chris and Jack are pseudonyms.
7 The following is a personal anecdote by one of the authors.
8 The following is a personal anecdote by one of the authors.

DOI: 10.1057/9781137351845

References

Allington, R. L. (2008). *What Really Matters in Response to Intervention: Research-based Designs*. Boston: Allyn & Bacon.

Clark, R. (2011). *The End of Molasses Classes: Getting our Kids Unstuck—101 Extraordinary Solutions for Parents and Teachers*. New York: Touchstone.

"Darling, W." (2002). "What 'No Child Left Behind' left behind". In L. Adler-Kassner (ed.), *Considering Literacy: Reading and Writing the Educational Experience* (pp. 313–318). New York: Pearson Education, Inc.

Esquith, R. (2007). *Teach Like your Hair's on Fire: The Methods and Madness Inside Room 56*. New York: Penguin Group.

Huot, B. (2002). *(Re)articulating Writing Assessment for Teaching and Learning*. Logan: Utah State University Press.

Kozol, J. (2005). *The Shame of a Nation: The Restoration of Apartheid Schooling in America*. New York: Crown.

Lortie, D. C. (1975). *Schoolteacher*. Chicago: University of Chicago Press.

National Center for Education Statistics (2009). *The Nation's Report Card: Reading 2009* (NCES 2010–458). Washington: Institute of Education Sciences, US Department of Education.

Ravitch, D. (2010). *The Death and Life of the Great American School System: How Testing and Choice Are Undermining Education*. New York: Basic Books.

Traub, J. (2002). "The test mess". In L. Adler-Kassner (ed.), *Considering Literacy: Reading and Writing the Educational Experience* (pp. 339–352). New York: Pearson Education, Inc.

DOI: 10.1057/9781137351845

4

Early Childhood Education

Kathleen Buehler, Kelsie Corriston, Emily Franz, Meredith Holland, Allison Marchesani, and Maggie O'Brien with Maria K. McKenna

Abstract: *This chapter focuses on early childhood education as an important facet of educational reform. Student authors assert that early childhood education is a necessary intervention for closing the proverbial achievement gap. Specifically, the chapter argues that early childhood education is a meaningful means of re-mediating the differences, often attributed to varying parenting and child-rearing circumstances, in children's readiness for the narrowly tailored, high stakes, middle class minded testing environment of formal schooling. The Authors rely on personal/anecdotal evidence interspersed with academic research supporting the efficacy of early learning. Finally, the authors use a select group of case study vignettes to highlight successful early childhood interventions.*

Collier, Brian S, McKenna, Maria K. and Burke, Kevin J. *College Student Voices on Educational Reform: Challenging and Changing Conversations.* New York: Palgrave Macmillan, 2013. DOI: 10.1057/9781137351845.

Foreword

This student-authored chapter demonstrates the natural complexity of education as a discipline. It is circuitous and at times repetitive. It elucidates the interdisciplinary nature of education, recognizes the longevity of the educational process (*aka life*), and challenges the reader to examine the personal lens through which s/he views the educational process. Education is by its very nature multilayered—our students recognize this but at times aren't sure how to deal with this fact. Children grow and develop, albeit in different ways, inside and out of the formal schooling process. As our student authors come to realize this complexity they quasi-adeptly, and appropriately we think, expand their definition of schooling in useful ways. In this chapter, although limited in specificity beyond "best practice" examples, we see that growth. Most importantly, we see value in the student writing because of its inclusive and pragmatically broad view of education reform. By selecting early childhood education as one of the three pillars to focus on in this text and then looking to "best practices" to find answers for the larger whole we see students appreciate collaboration, agency, and critical thinking. Reformers, educators, and students can read this chapter with an eye toward imagining the process these students took to write about their reform ideas, reflecting on their own personal histories, and thinking through how to look at "best practices" in useful ways for education reform.

Growing

In the broadest sense, this text begins with the end in mind. Our work together in this course and the students' writing was certainly about allowing space for a variety of voices on education reform to emerge. More importantly though, along with this aim, comes the bigger, and we believe, communal work of envisioning what must "be" in the world to improve the educational process for all children. In this chapter, we see the value in this type of work emerge on two levels. First, we note the dichotomy of students coming to terms with the frustrating complexity of education while also remaining hopeful (or stuck as some might see it) about somewhat traditional interventions, including beefing up early childhood education, as a means to a better end. Second, we see conversations about the purpose of education—and, importantly, a starting

DOI: 10.1057/9781137351845

point for unpacking stereotypes, biases, even erroneous thinking in some cases—emerge in this text. These conversations come about not in the artificial way that assignments or conversations in educationally designed experiences do—but in a natural, reflexive way independent of the rhetoric of any particular course, *(F)*forum, or individual instructor. Certainly, the reader might see these aspects of the students' education and experience come out in their suggestions but we also recognize the students' collective, and perhaps not yet completely coherent, philosophy of education materialize. This chapter allows these students to own their ideas—for better and worse. Here again, we are reminded of Bakhtin's (1994) notion of "ideological becoming" and the deep, uncomfortable work of "coming to know" that Britzman (2003) eloquently refers to in her writing.

This work also reflects the fact that our students are the beneficiaries of many of the policies and ideas that they propose as reform models for education. Many, if not all, of these students were blessed with familial and environmental circumstances which allowed for positive interactions with early learning. As one student noted early on in the course:

> *I'm a huge fan of early childhood education as an attempt to improve educational attainment. I think it gets kids familiar with the idea of school as a fun, safe, place where learning happens* (read: her own experience with early childhood education was safe, fun, and full of learning). *I also think it may offset some of the early differences between children in poverty and children in middle/upperclass households.*[1]

To some degree, for everyone involved, the endeavor of envisioning educational reform necessitates (re)constructing an idealized vision of our own academic history and building educational policy that is aided (or limited as the case may be) by this mostly personal, narrative construction. In order to make sense of our personal academic successes (or failures) thus far we must believe that some of what we experience(d) within our educational experiences was valuable and, perhaps, necessary for others to flourish (Goodlad, 1992; Strauss, 2010). In this way, our students are no different. They come to believe, first via reflection and later in searching for the evidence to support their beliefs in the writing below, that these opportunities might also be valuable components of traditional school reform writ large. We see this writing as a stop along the way—a work in progress—not to be read as an over-simplification of possible educational interventions but as both a viable set of options for reform *and* a point of reflection along the way that all educational reformers must accept as part of the process.

DOI: 10.1057/9781137351845

The complexity of our society *and* the complexities of learning require deep, multifaceted exploration of phenomena/cases/circumstances from those "doing" the work of education. As we see the students model here, reformers should be willing to become familiar with and be forthcoming about the lenses that they bring to research, policy, and pedagogy for true change to take hold (Glesne, 2006; Goodlad, 1992; Greene and Tucker, 2011; Ravitch, 2010). Thus, this chapter illuminates an important facet of educational reform with their written "self-talk" (a facet we believe many current reformers would be prudent to spend some time working through).

Researchers at Harvard's Center on the Developing Child state, "Early experiences affect the quality of the architecture of the brain by establishing either a sturdy or a fragile foundation for all of the learning, health and behavior that follows" (National Scientific Council on the Developing Child (NSCDC, 2012). This powerful reminder of the value of early learning-opportunities highlights the importance of early childhood experience and parallels the rationale of our work here as reflexive practitioners. By working to establish "architecture" that allows for the possibility of growth and open thinking in the discursive process with/for our students we mirror the belief that a "sturdy foundation" whether biological or metaphorical is imperative to development. As such, we also open ourselves up to the possibility that the ideas presented in this chapter are, in fact, still developing and encourage you to do the same.

As the reader will see, our students are working and re-working the edges of existing practices, their own experiences, and idealized notions of childcare and early childhood education. One notable absence in this chapter is any nuanced discussion of parenting and familial practices, beyond the discussion regarding distinctions of parenting styles that often accompanies economic stratification. The writers understand examining and incorporating parenting practices, cultural difference, and attention to home-school connections as part of formal early childhood discourse but aren't sure how to look at this from anything but a "deficit laden" perspective. The ideas presented in this chapter are at a hopeful, if not somewhat impatient, stage of educational thinking. Temple Grandin, notable animal science expert and autism awareness advocate, made the phrase, "different not less" famous.[2] This phrase strikes a chord as a useful way in which to examine this work. We invite you to reflect on your own pre-suppositions and positions related to early childhood education *and* students (adults or children) as "experts" while you move through this chapter and think about how it is "different not less."

DOI: 10.1057/9781137351845

Introduction

In her lecture at Notre Dame in 2012, Diane Ravitch commented on the power of education to remediate many societal issues. She advocated strengthening literacy skills, and a more humane understanding and application of standardized testing. Like Ravitch, we believe, as a nation, we[3] must invest in our children. Giving children the help that they need, especially early on, is an expensive proposition but is an investment that is worth making. Ravitch agrees saying, "there are so many things that we could do to make the lives of children better" (personal communication, April 10, 2012). Related to this, we believe that early childhood education, both through family involvement and preschool, is essential to child development and the formal educational process. When civil society fails to recognize the importance of early childhood education, as evidenced by a lack of support for local school districts trying to implement early childhood programming or funding cuts to programs that some of our youngest and most vulnerable need the most, we implicitly admit that we have not yet fully accepted responsibility for our youth. We struggle to incorporate differences arising from race and socioeconomic status into the educational process. This also impacts our youth. There is a devaluation of the children throughout our nation as evidenced by our inattentiveness to educational equity, especially in terms of early childhood programming and access. It is the gravest of moral sins and demands our complete attention.

To address our beliefs regarding early childhood education, it is important to begin with an understanding of the current state of early childhood education in the United States. From there we will transition to our hopeful ideas found in concrete examples of exemplary programs that "make the lives of children better." In light of these programs, we conclude with a reflection on the crucial features of high-quality preschool and daycare.

This we believe

We believe that early childhood education is the foundation of schooling for children and an opportunity to shape every student's sense of agency and engagement in learning. Many resilient and talented children will fail because they have different kinds of social or cultural capital than formal schooling demands. Some will drop out of high school altogether, others

DOI: 10.1057/9781137351845

will receive a GED rather than a diploma; many will accept a wage that will not prove sustainable. If public education is to serve as the great American equalizer, certain inequities must be addressed within the system. Our current educational system does not translate the principle of equal access into equal outcomes, which means that simply expanding our public education system to include pre-kindergarten programming is not enough. Structural change must occur in order to address established inequities. Furthermore, we must question whether access is indeed equal if the quality of available programs is not. Individuals can learn from adversity, the pressure of fight or flight. And our work here begs the question "at what point does an institution/system systematically encourage certain kids, those with less, those who might need more, those who don't quite fit to 'fight'"? You could ask this question a different way by wondering, is our educational system successful if it is mostly middle and upper class children who consistently succeed within the given framework?

We believe early childhood education is fundamental to a child's social and cognitive development. Current state systems establish that the right to public education begins between five and eight-years of age depending on the state. If we believe early learning is important why should a child only claim his or her right after an arbitrarily determined age? If the years before kindergarten are formative—as studies have shown—then formal education before kindergarten does have a role to play in our national education policy.

Prior to formal schooling, children are largely shaped by the development and socialization that occurs in the home. This means that the family, defined by its demographic and economic features, directly impacts the way children develop during early childhood, particularly prior to their entry into formal educational institutions. The family is the primary space for learning. Differences in socioeconomic status, family environment, and the resources available in the home create substantial and measurable gaps in school readiness, vocabulary, and other critical factors for school performance (Rothstein, 2004). Thus, economic factors not only impact the likelihood of a successful beginning school experience but also the other opportunities available to children before they become "formal" students.

We believe that access to early childhood programs is a necessity rather than a luxury. Accessible early childhood programs are good for child development and allow parents, particularly mothers, to make the choice whether to return to work; without publicly supported programs

DOI: 10.1057/9781137351845

many parents have no other option but to stay home with their children. Early childhood programs offer children opportunities for socialization and educational development, but they also have the potential to foster more positive parent–child relationships at home providing an avenue to parental education programs. Furthermore, early childhood education can serve as a vehicle for addressing inequities that arise from the socioeconomic gap which later impact the achievement gap.

Socialization processes differ between socioeconomic classes. Lareau (2002) found that middle class parents engage in what she calls, "concerted cultivation" while working and lower class parents foster "natural growth." Concerted cultivation entails a sense of emerging entitlement and organized, detailed involvement in a child's life. Children are provided lessons, after school activities, and a great deal of adult–child interaction. These children, Lareau (2002) asserts, have a sense of their own agency and high self-efficacy in different circumstances. Children are taught how to interact with authority figures and their skill-set feeds into the skills formal schooling requires of children. Natural growth, on the other hand, fosters obedience but also independent play and thinking. Children who grow up in an environment of "natural growth" are more likely to fear and obey authoritative figures, such as school officials and other professionals, without question. They have fewer of the skills school tends to value but a great deal of "street" or "common sense" intelligence. This paradox often leads to a deficit model of thinking about different upbringings especially since natural growth is more prevalent in families of low socioeconomic status. Therefore, we must recognize that class differences create various cultural logics that provide disparate resources.

Again, this does not suggest that one type of child-rearing is superior. Rather just that schooling seems to reward one over the other. Therefore, the abilities of children are not viewed as equal even as they enter formal schooling for the first time in kindergarten; their environments and experiences before this age contribute to discrepancies in each child's prior knowledge.

Flaws of the system

The concept of "the system," is abstract. As American students we have experience with the realities of American schooling. We also recognize, as students at a selective university, we have ostensibly "succeeded" at

DOI: 10.1057/9781137351845

making it through the system, from kindergarten through high school graduation and beyond. The smoothness and uniformity of individual educational paths varies and almost always includes times of struggle, yet somehow many students do find their way to the flowing robes, tasseled hats, and diplomas. High school diplomas are validations, not prizes, for high achieving students. Receiving them seems like a rite of passage, an emotional experience, but also one that is expected for many of us. Those of us who made it through the system with this mindset are, after all, success stories. In our privileged worlds, failing to graduate from high school is inconceivable and college attendance is an assumed "next step." The truth is though, that the assumption is not true for everyone in the system (Allensworth and Easton, 2005; Tough, 2008).

The questions remain: *why*, and perhaps more importantly *how*, do some students succeed in school while others fail? More vital for this chapter is the question: how does future academic success relate to early childhood education? Cultural, social, and economic factors are important aspects of these questions. Race, ethnicity, socioeconomic status, parental education levels, and many other factors create opportunities that enable success in a bureaucratic, educational system based on uniformity and structural authority (Rothstein, 2004; Yosso, 2005). Recent data from the National Center for Children in Poverty suggests that toddlers as young as two from lower income households already lag behind their better-off peers in traditional cognitive and behavioral performances and struggle to catch up without early intervention (Robbins, Stagman, and Smith, 2012). By virtue of factors outside of any one individual's control, many children obtain cultural currency along the path of life that is useful in the schooling process (Yosso, 2005). We recognize as current students of higher education, our own success within the educational system, came at least partially because of our cultural and social capital. We "know" how the system works.

Unfortunately, the current system does not work for everyone. Early childhood education has some power to change this fact. To begin, it is useful to clarify just what early childhood education means. Mitchell, Ripple, and Chanana (1998) note:

> Early childhood policy aims to ensure that all children come to school ready to succeed and that families are supported as parents and as essential participants in the workforce. A comprehensive policy framework would include special education for preschoolers and for infants, toddlers and their families; elementary education; childcare for young children as well as school-age children.

DOI: 10.1057/9781137351845

In the United States, early childhood/pre-kindergarten programs are not a consistent nor are they a robust aspect of comprehensive, state funded public education (Barnett et al., 2011; Mitchell, Ripple and Chanana, 1998; NEA, 2011). Currently, all 50 states offer some form of state funded early childhood education. However, these programs are limited in breadth. Across the nation, on average, state funded preschool reaches only about 28% of four-year olds and only 12% of all American three- and four-year-olds combined (AFT, 2008; Barnett et al., 2011; NEA, 2011). While promising strides were made in the promotion and funding for early childhood education during the first decade of the 21st century, it is again, sadly, losing ground in political and policy circles. As a result, parents who are able, simply send their children to private day-care programs or attend "pay for service" preschools. Some programs, such as Head Start, offer subsidized tuition for low-income families. It is, however, woefully underfunded. As a result, in the absence of a free public educational option for early childhood education, the vast majority of individuals must hire childcare, rely on relatives, or stay home to care for their own children.

Socioeconomic factors undoubtedly influence the type and scope of opportunities related to a child's development. During the zero-to-six stage of development, it is especially true that the parenting and educational choices of many families are influenced by income. As a consequence, once children are in the formal education system, there is not a level playing field. Some children have access to resources that others lack, not because of ability, mind you, but because of how income influences socialization and early education processes. Financial resources translate into social capital, which fosters additional advantages over other children with less social capital (Coleman, 1987). With this work we seek to challenge the status quo, recognizing the importance of implementing a system of free, universal, early childhood-education programs across the United States and providing examples of "best practice" from a variety of angles.

A model from afar: "a you pick two" example

Examining international examples of public education highlights programs and structures that might be considered for implementation in the United States.

DOI: 10.1057/9781137351845

Governments throughout the world, but especially in Europe, have family friendly government and business policies from birth promoting early education, helping both children and working parents. By way of example, over 163 nations fund paid maternity leave; over 70 countries protect the right of working women to breastfeeding by law; almost 50 countries guarantee fathers the right to paternity leave (Heymann, as cited in Widener, 2007). The US does none of these things.[4] Here it is useful to provide some specific comparisons when considering comparing early childhood credential requirements between France and the United States. Preschool teachers in France are required to have a teaching credential and Masters degree and are paid accordingly (Clawson and Gerstel, 2002). By contrast, there are no legal prerequisites for teaching in early childhood programs in the United States.

Related to this, nearly 100% of French children aged three to five are enrolled in *ecoles maternelles*, the country's nationalized early education program, where the primary goal is school readiness. Even non-working parents enroll their children in the programs because of the educational and developmental benefits (Clawson and Gerstel, 2002). By way of contrast, in the United States in 2010, only 15% of children ages zero to four living in poverty were in center-based daycares, while 26% of children in families above the poverty line were enrolled in center-based daycares (Federal Interagency Forum on Child and Family Statistics, 2011).

We see early childhood programs like the *ecoles maternelles* and highly qualified teachers as ideal for a national early childhood education program. The ability for all children to attend the same type of high-quality institution changes opportunities for each individual moving forward. However, examining examples or pieces of early childhood programs outside of the US has its limitations. America's schooling system is unique and quite a bit more complicated than some other nations, including France. Geographic size, diversity, and a long history of issues stemming from strained race relations fundamentally impact our growth and our education policies. We also need to more fully devote attention to advocating within our current system for opportunities to better serve the needs of today's students and parents. This can be accomplished by attending to the well-respected research on the benefits of early childhood education which, while valuable, is not what we elected to spend our time writing on. We are already convinced of the value of early childhood education and hope to demonstrate a forward thinking approach to possibilities in this field.[5]

DOI: 10.1057/9781137351845

Hope close to home: exemplary early childhood examples in the United States

Interventions through early childhood education are an essential component to closing the "achievement gap" that is already present on the first day of kindergarten (Barnett, Carolan, Fitzgerald, and Squires, 2011; Rothstein, 2004). For children who are raised in family situations that cannot provide access to the many resources needed to encourage their cognitive and social development in the manner that formal American schooling demands, a safe, educational environment is essential.

Across the country, thousands of successful early childhood interventions occur every day. To demonstrate the positive possibility of these interventions, we will highlight three programs. The Dolores Kohl Education Foundation's Story Bus in Chicago, Illinois—a museum on wheels that promotes fun and active learning with an emphasis on literacy—is a creative example of a community partnership in early childhood education. Second, the Harlem Children's Zone is well-known for its education interventions that work to stop the vicious cycle of poverty. Finally, the mission of Focus on Renewal's "Positive Parenting Program" in McKees Rocks, Pennsylvania seeks to prevent child abuse through the Parents as Teachers Curriculum (PAT), home visits, and free preschool programs. Notably, in each case, the programs we highlight are community/foundation based initiatives not federal or state programs. This is important. Our work in this chapter does advocate for federal and/or state programming and sees early childhood education as a piece of the free, public education we as a nation have agreed to provide children in the United States. We are not taking up the specifics of how this is to be done on a larger scale but instead use these examples to highlight programs that are notable for their success and attention to elements of child development, community growth, and cohesion between children, families, and educational entities. We do not want people to re-invent the wheel, rather we suggest looking at programs that are working and building or adapting ideas from these spaces.

The Dolores Kohl Education Foundation Story Bus

In Chicago, Illinois, the Dolores Kohl Education Foundation[6]strives to enhance early childhood education in underprivileged neighborhoods

DOI: 10.1057/9781137351845

by promoting literacy skills through its story-based preschool and kindergarten curriculum, along with the "children's museum on wheels that acts as a culminating event to [the] curriculum" (Story Bus, 2012). The program, called Story Bus, emphasizes respect for the role of both teachers and children in the learning experience and works with children through local schools. This respect is facilitated through four Story Bus stories, which encourage students to experience reading through engaging activities:

> The program empowers teachers by encouraging them to develop their own curriculum, teaching to the whole child, utilizing a single classic story. It enables young students to have collaborative literary experiences that bring stories to life, so that they better understand the stories. (Story Bus, 2012)

Programs such as Story Bus provide the opportunity to intervene in a child's environment and begin to develop children's literacy skills in a memorable way. The Story Bus program is one way to serve children who are "missing crucial early literacy experiences that can determine their lifetime success" (Story Bus, 2012). Community based efforts are essential in the United States' current education environment. The visible presence of this outreach in locations where early childhood education is not universally available allows for needed exposure to children, parents, and community members.

Harlem Children's Zone: Harlem Gems

We find another successful program in Geoffrey Canada's visionary attempt to blanket an area with a "wrap-around" intervention. The Harlem Children's Zone (HCZ) is well-known for its innovative approach to education and interrupting cycles of generational poverty. One program offered by the organization, Harlem Gems, works to prepare children for kindergarten while integrating the whole family into its approach to early learning.

The program provides all-day pre-kindergarten to families that live, work, or go to school within the geographical zone it serves, for free. The child-to-adult ratio is 4:1, allowing teachers to devote personal attention to each child. The program lasts from 8 a.m. to 6 p.m., allowing parents to work and requires an investment of time and parent education from the families using the program. The Harlem Children's Zone currently

DOI: 10.1057/9781137351845

operates three sites and serves over 200 children each year (Harlem Children's Zone, 2008). The program is not the typical pre-kindergarten environment. Rather, its mission is to educate the whole child and the whole family, meaning that the children each receive an individualized education and parents are incorporated into their child's experience.[7] One of the goals of the program is, naturally, to prepare children for entry into kindergarten.

Many families enter Harlem Gems after participating in Baby College, another HCZ program. The children then continue onto HCZ schools, creating continuity in their education. Children learn three languages (English, Spanish, and French), but not all have English as a first-language. This means that Harlem Gems provides second language instruction to all of its pupils while still encouraging ties to their native culture as bilingual education advocates suggest (Robledo and Cortez, 2001). Children are tested through entrance and exit assessments, allowing teachers to develop individual education plans and track student progress.

In addition, the program also promotes social learning. Children need to develop their cognitive, emotional, and social skills. This is facilitated through small group interaction, possible because of the low adult–child ratio, and staff are trained to better encourage these areas of development. The program is currently working with Columbia University to develop and sustain emotionally responsive classrooms. Members of the HCZ staff have been trained to use consistent language and find positive ways to communicate with children. The program's greatest strengths include its emphasis on individual attention, continuity of services through HCZ, and the "safe, stable, clean classrooms that provide a consistent routine" (Harlem Children's Zone, 2008). This consistency and focus on the whole child provides a safe zone for the Gems of Harlem to develop, both as children and as students. The program's services do not end with the education of children. Rather, the program also works to educate families. Recognizing the importance of parents in a child's development, Harlem Gems offers a parent participation program called Head Start. The goal is for parents to become active participants in their children's education, often by seeing the world from their child's point-of-view.

A child is not a little adult: he or she requires care and attention. At the same time, children's needs, wants, and opinions should not be dismissed. So often our educational system demeans its students: they must

DOI: 10.1057/9781137351845

only ever sit straight at their desks, listen to the teacher, and conform to classroom expectations. Children who deviate become "poor students"; those who can meet expectations are "good students." Our society proposes that all children have something to offer, yet our strict system of physical, intellectual, and social constraints fails to foster the unique value of each child as a free-thinking individual. The Harlem Gem program seems to respect children and acknowledge inherent abilities that can be encouraged through education. Not only does the program recognize the potential of the children, it also incorporates low-income parents into an established system that, as Lareau (2002) notes, tends to favor the middle class. This works to mitigate for poor and working class parents, what can be an intimidating and often unnavigable system of public education.

Does the program work? According to the HCZ, 16.5% of four-year olds entering the program in the 2009–2010 school year had school readiness classifications of delayed or very delayed. By the end of the year, none of the children remained "very delayed." Furthermore, 99.5% of students had a readiness of average or above. The children, according to these statistics, are prepared for entry into kindergarten. Perhaps the greatest "gem" of the program lies in the HCZ's higher educational goal "from Harlem to Harvard." HCZ makes education and positive cognitive, social, and emotional learning accessible to families who lack the social and financial capital to provide those resources due to their socio-economic status (Harlem Children's Zone, 2008).

Focus on renewal: positive parenting program

In McKees Rocks, Pennsylvania, one priest, many employees, and an army of advocates have been struggling for decades to transform a community. Father Regis Ryan supports some of the poorest individuals living on the fringes of society through Focus on Renewal (FOR), a community organization that provides a variety of services.[8] One day a week, residents can come to the community center, located in the town's former bank, for food from the food pantry. Every day, members of the community can come for support, conversation, a free clinic, hot lunch, and whatever else they need.

One exemplary program in FOR takes place from 9 a.m. to noon, Monday through Friday in the basement of the bank building. Children

DOI: 10.1057/9781137351845

aged three to five attend "Positive Parenting Preschool," a free program where the children participate in school readiness and social activities. The children learn letters and numbers through games. They are encouraged to respect the teachers, learning to sit quietly while books are read. Social development is facilitated through peer interaction, as children play with their classmates. The children also learn to take responsibility for themselves by putting toys away and cleaning up after snack time. For many children, these lessons are not easy, particularly if their home environment is unstructured or lacking in resources that allow them to be "ready" for this type of environment.

These interventions are successful in part due to the inclusion of a variety of support mechanisms that can assist the members of the community. First, the FOR educational program is only one piece of the larger community programming structure. Families have access to the food, meals, money, prayers, books, and activities coordinated by FOR. While these services are not always enough to give the children an experience equal to that of many middle class, suburban children, they can nonetheless improve the quality of life of many children living in "The Rocks." Second, the program provides the children with a structured experience. Consistency, the kind that often comes with affluence, exists sporadically for many of the children in FOR. The people in their lives are often absent, as parents and relatives struggle with incarceration and military deployment, both of which separate the children from their guardians. Further, many of the children move frequently, transitioning from homes to apartments or shelters, as their parents seek places to live. "Positive Parenting" offers a dependable, uniform experience; every time the children come to their classroom, they grow to trust that they will be greeted by encouraging adults and new learning experiences. Third, the program offers wrap-around services during school time, incorporating care of the children's health and well-being into their educational experience. For example, a dentist comes during school time to check the children's teeth, teach the children to care for their teeth, and distribute toothbrushes.

Fourth, the teachers make home visits in the afternoons. The goal of the Parents as Teachers (PAT) curriculum is to improve their students' home lives by educating their parents. These home visits attempt to bridge the gap between time spent in the classroom and at home, as differences in structure and resources create varied environments. As the students spend most of their day at home, creating a positive, safe,

DOI: 10.1057/9781137351845

learning environment at home is essential to encouraging strong early childhood development.

Finally, and perhaps most importantly, the FOR program accepts all children, with no restrictions. While this is the program's greatest challenge, it is also a great strength and great triumph in providing accessible early childhood education. FOR and its Positive Parenting Preschool are able to improve the lives of hundreds of people living in McKees Rocks through successful interventions that are supported by wrap-around services.

There are programs such as these across the nation. And our focus on this is personal. As authors who participate in community based learning courses, summer service opportunities, and ongoing service endeavors we've experienced some of these opportunities first hand. These experiences are most certainly part of how we have come to believe in the power of early childhood education. Upon reflection related to this experience, one of our authors writes:

> *One of my students had been kicked-out of several preschools for behavior problems. Although he was a very sweet boy on the inside, he did not know what to do with the complex emotions of frustration and anger that arose within himself. With structured discipline, courageous teaching, and my own special attention, the student's behavior improved dramatically during my eight weeks as a teacher in the program... Positive Parenting gave the student the chance to make improvements, grow, and learn.*

The Dolores Kohl Foundation's Story Bus, the Harlem Children's Zone Harlem Gems program, and Positive Parenting Preschool are three examples of how successful early childhood interventions can offer opportunity to many underprivileged children and continue to support those children with greater access to social, cultural, and economic opportunities. With programs like these children are given the chance to engage in learning environments that prepare them for kindergarten while also recognizing the importance of well-being of the "whole" child by providing additional wrap-around support services where necessary.

Key components of early childhood programming

> *When I was growing up, preschool seemed to function more as a daycare facility than as a place of educational enrichment. While the majority of people attended some sort of preschool, most were enrolled in the programs because of parent*

DOI: 10.1057/9781137351845

work schedules. The intent was not education, but rather attending to a variety of other needs, such as childcare.

This childhood experience of one of the authors is characteristic of many people throughout the country. However, recent trends demonstrate that there seems to be a renewed focus on making preschools more knowledge and learning focused. Researching the best educational practices, improving both teacher quality and training, refining curriculum, and implementing program evaluation make preschools and daycare facilities alike true educational environments that can truly impact the future academic performances of their students.. According to the National Education Association, studies such as the HighScope Perry Preschool Study and the Abecedarian Project indicate that children who have attended quality preschool programs are more likely to graduate from high school and earn more money late in life, to have longer marriages, and to own homes. Conversely, they are less likely to repeat grades, to require special education, and to run into trouble with the law. Unfortunately, as we've made clear, many daycare and preschool programs are a luxury, not available to all children, and many are not oriented toward education. Because of the demonstrated benefits of quality preschool programs, the NEA supports free, publicly funded, quality kindergarten programs in all states (National Education Association, 2011).

We assert that preschool and childcare facilities should be a place of both learning and growth, stimulating children's minds, and providing a formative social and emotional experience. For these reasons, we believe that the organization of early childhood education is important in fostering a positive and beneficial preschool education. First, it is essential to have the right teachers in the classroom. Early in childhood, children are malleable and can absorb information at intense rates. Thus, it is crucial that teachers are certified and capable of executing curriculum requirements. Second, curriculum must prepare children for the formal schooling environment. Given the way our educational system is set up at this time, it is necessary that children are exposed to letters, numbers, and reading before they enter grade school. In addition, proper licenses and routine evaluation of early childhood programs must be standard. These goals can be difficult to fulfill when a preschool is faced with funding issues and a lack of teachers, but should be recognized as important elements of early childhood education.

Finally, family involvement, or a lack thereof, is crucial in determining preschool outcomes. Encouraging children to explore and learn

DOI: 10.1057/9781137351845

while in the early stages of development and providing an environment supportive of such behavior greatly enhances the process of education. Prior to kindergarten, the environment of a child's intellectual development is largely provided by the child's family and the household in which the child lives. Having supportive parents who enroll their child in preschool and offer encouragement and assistance, in ways valued by schools, throughout those years is very important. Parents who recognize and embrace being deeply involved with the development of their children are better able to foster positive outcomes for early childhood development, encouraging both emotional and academic success for their children in the future.

An ideal learning environment: learning, creativity, (and order) in the classroom

Early childhood environments are designed to prepare children to enter their formal years of education. Their social development is also critical in helping ease their transition from preschool programs to the more structured environment of kindergarten. Children must learn how to interact with their peers, adults, and the classroom environment itself; these goals are most achievable in the setting of a classroom as other children and adult figures surround each student. As children expand their worlds beyond their immediate family and other avenues of narrow exposure social development is critical, as greater discipline, attention, and academic engagement are demanded.

In addition, every child must learn and engage with his or her peers. Developing communication skills is critical to the child's preparation. Early childhood classrooms should emphasize interaction with other students and respect for authority. Children should be encouraged to actively and respectfully express themselves through speaking, moving, and singing. Promoting a variety of activities is important in ensuring that every child will find the means of communication that best suits him. Offering opportunities for group communication, such as singing together, and individual communication, such as giving each child proper attention when he speaks or sings independently, is also important in fully developing their skills. Individual attention is particularly important as students can learn to express their personal emotions and experiences productively; this can be accomplished by having them tell

DOI: 10.1057/9781137351845

a story or describe their feelings. Encouraging the students to share both with one another and with teachers is also an important balance that must be achieved in developing their communication skills.

Children are also expected to interact with their environment. Early childhood education should serve as exposure to the proper behavior for more formal schooling. Listening skills, communication skills, respect for other students' personal space and feelings are all abstract capabilities that early childhood programs should address. However, there are more concrete practices that can also be carried from elementary education to preschool programs. Children can learn to raise their hands, be encouraged to ask questions, and know how to engage in both active independent learning and group activities. These abilities can be implemented in every early childhood classroom, offering better preparation for every child as they move toward formal schooling.

Along with socialization, the equally important aspect of character development within the classroom needs to be addressed. Children's minds are most malleable at this early stage of their life; this is the time when they look up to those surrounding them, repeating actions seen and words heard. In order to help guide these children into motivated and determined students, we must provide them with a positive and supportive environment in which to grow and succeed.

The self-esteem of each child matters and impacts their well-being. When students view themselves in a more positive light with higher worth, they are more likely to feel motivated and to succeed. This is especially important in education; as their formal schooling continues, students are given more independence and the need for drive and personal motivation increases. The role self-esteem plays in early childhood education is important in shaping the student's view of their personal capabilities from an early age. When they feel successful in school and have higher self-esteem, children are more likely to engage in educational opportunities and challenge themselves in unique ways. As such, early childhood education is important to buoy children's self-esteem.

As children's self-awareness and abilities positively increase, so too should the standard to which they are held. This drive from educators and parents helps students engage in their work. Though early childhood education programs should always hold young students to reasonable standards, giving children a goal to work for serves as positive reinforcement and allows the students to challenge themselves to learn and grow. We must start children on this positive path beginning with

DOI: 10.1057/9781137351845

their early childhood education. We want our students to be confident in their abilities and to strive for an autonomy that reinforces this attitude, promoting a positive cycle.

From the time they enter schooling, whether formal or informal, children are often "hardwired" or primed to think, act, and learn in a certain manner. For some, this may mean adhering to all rules and desires of teachers and parents, viewing school strictly as a place to gain the knowledge needed to succeed. This regimented aspect of schooling, while helpful in moving the student on to the next step, does not engage them in the educational process. They may indeed learn how to solve problems given to them in a textbook and develop test-taking skills, but children will ultimately lack the full experience of the essence of school, exploration and the development of creativity. For others, the educational process may be entirely social, as students may think that if they are being forced to go to school, they should simply forget the academic portion and simply do what they desire, interacting with their peers. These types of students often feel forced into an educational system that does not complement their dispositions or development to this point.

Precisely because of the diversity of children, early childhood programs should shift their focus, allowing the student to determine what school means through increased autonomy. This can be accomplished in a positive manner by presenting the child with less scripted ways of thinking and acting, while providing them with spaces and opportunities to foster their creativity. One of our chapter authors writes:

> *As a young child, I attended a Montessori preschool. Looking back, I feel very fortunate to have been enrolled in such a program because this type of learning really fostered my creativity in ways beyond that of other early schooling programs. Montessori education emphasizes learning through all five senses, quite a valuable experience for a young child.*

According to the architects of the Third Teacher movement (2010), "The senses are the gateway to the mind, particularly the developing mind... Sound, smell, taste, touch, and movement power memory. An environment rich in sensory experiences helps students retain and retrieve what they learn." This notion of fostering creativity through the senses is crucial in a young child's learning environment to help engage them in their surroundings. Tuan (1977) elaborates, "The five senses constantly reinforce each other to provide the intricately ordered and emotion-charged world in which we learn" (p. 11). Ultimately, the five

DOI: 10.1057/9781137351845

senses play a large role in shaping our experiences. Children should be a part of an early childhood education program that allows the senses to be explored and celebrated, thus offering a positive experience.

Aside from the importance of fostering creativity, children should also be held to some particular standard in coming to an understanding of basic skills and knowledge. In creating a more academic setting, preschools and other early education centers should continue to focus on preparing their students for the formal schooling that lies ahead of them. This is important to address so that children will not fall behind or feel underprepared when entering the next stage of their educational development. Teaching and learning basic skills is equally important to the task of these programs, so it is vital that they retain this focus and objective goal. Nonetheless, it remains important that this be achieved in an active and intriguing manner, integrating creativity and self-motivated exploration.

In an early childhood classroom, students should be engaged and feel a desire to learn. By encouraging this outlook from a young age when children are still forming their opinions, preschool can positively impact their future development as well. Early childhood education programs should strive to achieve this creative balance. We must allow children to explore and become engrossed in something, help children find a passion, and give children numerous opportunities to discover themselves in a formal-schooled setting. Importantly, these programs can transform the definition of teaching and learning, bringing about a positive understanding that education can and should be *fun*.

Conclusion

The intervention of a successful and encouraging early childhood program can certainly influence a child in many ways: he or she may realize great individual value and potential, become infatuated with exploration and self-motivated learning, or become well equipped with necessary social and behavioral skills. Preschool programming can introduce children to the basics of learning and socialization that may not be present in their homes. However, we must remember that preschool is not a "corrector," but a supplement to the developmental process. Making sure each child knows the alphabet and how to raise his hand to show he needs attention is possible, but encouraging each child

DOI: 10.1057/9781137351845

to fully embrace learning and creative endeavors is not always achievable, particularly when there is not an atmosphere of support at home. In other words, resources and exposure can be supplemented, but the culture of early childhood education does not negate the culture of the home in which the child lives. Preschool can be a transformative experience for some, but not all. One child may go home to an environment directed toward development and learning, while another may return to a lack of emotional, financial, or academic resources. Early childhood education is important in addressing preparation for formal schooling; we must ensure that every child develops strong social skills, encourage the development of their character, engage their love of exploration and creativity, and expose each child to foundational academic knowledge. We believe that these aims are achievable, but we also recognize that this is not a solution. We must also continue to address what happens when children return home; looking toward the issues of poverty, poorly educated parents, and the lack of community and social capital that is valued by our educational system. We must learn to value cultural difference and shore up skills that allow children access and success within the educational process. Only when these issues are also addressed can successful early childhood interventions truly begin to transform the lives and prospects of our children. As one of us wrote in a journal entry for this course:

> *Although I attended preschool for a year before entering kindergarten, I see my early childhood experience as largely being formed by my life at home. Both of my parents have been extremely active in my education and development as a person throughout my entire life, and their attention during my early childhood years was particularly important in cultivating my appreciation and love of learning. My mom chose to stay at home with my sister and me, and this constant presence was an incredible gift to which I attribute much of my academic success and personal growth. Our home was filled with arts and crafts projects and music to facilitate creativity, puzzles and games to foster problem solving, and books to help us learn to love to read and explore. I attended art and dance classes and took music lessons before I entered kindergarten. I honestly never realized that this intense devotion to our development was such a conscious effort and not present in every child's home until I was much older. Many of our activities and resources are clearly a result of my family's economic security and ability to devote both time and finances to our development and education, but I believe that my parents' deep attention and the values they worked to instill in my sister and me were the most critical aspects of our childhoods.*

DOI: 10.1057/9781137351845

Reading Other People's Words by Victoria Purcell-Gates made clear to me the extreme discrepancy between my experience and that of many other children. This text describes an Urban Appalachia family raising two children in a completely illiterate home (Purcell-Gates, 1995). Though the mother did her best, her personal resources were not conducive to raising children that could be successful in the educational system that exists. She did not send her children to kindergarten because she didn't know about the program and was unable to establish or maintain any sort of relationship with the schools because of her illiteracy. That such communities exist—ones lacking not only financial resources but also personal resources (i.e. those resources that provide an individual with the tools to navigate a narrowly tailored system)—is both shocking and disheartening. My personal story is different not only because of my family's ability to invest a great amount of money in my growth and education, but also because great knowledge and personal resources enhanced the attention that they devoted to my sister and me. I am realizing that we can no longer classify early childhood development (only) by socioeconomic status or a child's participation in a specific program; the parents and their ability to be involved and serve their children are integral aspects of this part of a child's development that cannot be dictated by a policy nor corrected by funding. We must find a way to meld all of the formative elements into every child's early childhood experience so that each child receives the experience that I was fortunate enough to have in every way.

And with that, we have come full circle and end with a useful reminder, "If in interpretive phenomenology" (*the act of interpreting a given phenomenon, in our case educational reform*):

> Discourse always requires a presence of a hearer or reader to form its meaning—then its writing must also preserve openness or incompleteness. In this regard, a reflective discourse does not struggle for ultimate clarity; it does not wish to arrive at a reductive point for agreement. Instead it seeks to elicit a dialogue between author and reader and further to initiate reflective thought in the reader. (Darroch and Silvers, 1984, p. 191)

Notes

1 All student quotes come from written reflections, journaling, and/or transcribed classroom conversations over the eight-month course.

2 For more on Temple Grandin see; Grandin, T. (2011). "The Way I See It", Revised and Expanded 2nd edition: *A Personal Look at Autism and Asperger's*, 2nd ed. Arlington, TX: Future Horizons.

3 From here on "we" refers to the student authors of the chapter.

DOI: 10.1057/9781137351845

4 Jody Heymann, founder of Global Working Families and director of Institute for Health and Social Policy at McGill University provides a robust understanding of family friendly policies around the globe in her work through the GWF.
5 See the Harvard Family Research Project at http://www.hfrp.org/early-childhood-education for a broad overview of support for expanding early childhood education in the United States.
6 For more information on this program and organization see www.dkef.org and www.storybus.org.
7 For more about this approach see: Kumar, R., Gheen, M. H. and Kaplan, A. (2002). "Goal structures in the learning environment and students' disaffection from learning and schooling." In C. Midgley (ed.), *Goals, Goal Structures, and Patterns of Adaptive Learning* (pp. 142–173). Hillsdale, New Jersey: Erlbaum.
8 For more information on Focus on Renewal visit: www.forstorox.org.

References

American Federation of Teachers (2008). "At the starting line: Early childhood education in the 50 states". Retrieved from: http://www.aft.org/pdfs/ece/startingline1200.pdf.

Allensworth, E. and Easton, J. (2005). "The on-track indicator as a predictor of high school graduation". *Consortium on Chicago School Research*. Chicago, IL, USA: University of Chicago.

Bakhtin, M. (1994). *The Bakhtinian Reader: Selected Writings of Bakhtin, Medvedev*. Voloshinov (ed). London: Edward Arnold.

Barnett, W., Carolan, M., Fitzgerald, J., and Squires, J. (2011). *The State of Preschool 2011: State Preschool Yearbook*. New Brunswick, New Jersey: National Institute for Early Education Research.

Britzman, D. (2003). *Practice Makes Practice: A Critical Study of Learning to Teach*. Albany, NY, USA: State University of New York Press.

Clawson, D. and Gerstel, N. (2002). "Caring for our young: child care in Europe and the United States". *Contexts*. 1, pp. 28–35.

Coleman, J. (1987). "Social capital and the development of youth". *Momentum*. 18(4), pp. 6–8.

Darroch, V. and Silvers, R. (1984). "The language of description and theorizing in reflective discourse". *Phenomenology and Pedagogy*. 2(2), pp. 191–194.

Federal Interagency Forum on Child and Family Statistics. (2011). America's Children: Key National Indicators of Well-Being 2011. *Childstats*.

DOI: 10.1057/9781137351845

gov. Retrieved from: http://www.childstats.gov/americaschildren/famsoc3.asp.
Glesne, C. (2006). *Becoming Qualitative Researchers: An Introduction*. New York: Allyn & Bacon.
Goodlad, J. (1992). "On taking school reform seriously". *The Phi Delta Kappan*. 74(3), pp. 232–238.
Greene, M. and Tucker, J. (2011). "Tumultuous times of education reform: a critical reflection on caring in policy and practice". *International Journal of Leadership Education*. 14(1), pp. 1–19.
Harlem Children's Zone. (2008). Retrieved from http://www.hcz.org/programs/early-childhood.
Lareau, A. (2002). "Invisible inequality: social class and childrearing in black families and white families". *American Sociological Review*. 67(5), 747–776. Retrieved from http://search.proquest.com/docview/60085276?accountid=12874.
McClure, R. (2012). *Montessori Education*. Retrieved from http://childcare.about.com/cs/preschools/g/montessori.html.
Mitchell, A., Ripple, C., and Chanana, N. (1998). "Prekindergarten programs funded by the states: essential elements for policy makers". New York: Families and Work Institute.
National Education Association. (2011). "Early childhood education". Retrieved from http://www.nea.org/home/18163.htm.
National Scientific Council on the Developing Child. (2012). "In brief: the science of early childhood development". Retrieved from: developingchild.harvard.edu/download_file/-/view/64/OWP/P Architects, VS Furniture.
O'Donnell Wicklund Pigozzi and Peterson, Architects Inc., VS Furniture., and Bruce Mau Design. (2010). *The third teacher: 79 ways you can use design to transform teaching & learning*. New York: Abrams.
Purcell-Gates, V. (1995). *Other People's Words: The Cycle of Low Literacy*. Cambridge, MA: Harvard University Press.
Ravitch, D. (2010). *The Death and Life of the Great American School System*. New York, NY: Basic Books.
Robbins, T., Stagman, S. and Smith, S. (2012). "Practices for PromotingYoung Children's Learning in QRIS Standards". *National Center for Children in Poverty (NCCP)*. Retrieved from: http://www.nccp.org/publications/pdf/text_1070.pdf.
Robledo-Montecel, M. and Cortez, J. D. (2001). "Successful bilingual education programs: criteria for exemplary practices in bilingual

DOI: 10.1057/9781137351845

education". *IDRA Newsletter*. San Antonio, TX: Intercultural Development Research Association.
Rothstein, R. (2004). *Class and Schools: Using Social, Economic, and Educational Reform to Close the Black-White Achievement Gap*. Washington D.C: Economic Policy Institute.
Story Bus. (2012). *About Us*. Retrieved from: http://www.storybus.org/about.
Tough, P. (2008). *Whatever it Takes*. New York, NY: Houghton Mifflin.
Tuan, Y. (1977). *Space and Place: The Perspective of Experience*. St. Paul, MN: University of Minnesota Press.
Strauss, V. (2010). "Goodlad on school reform: are we ignoring lessons of last 50 years?" *The Washington Post*. Retrieved from http://voices.washingtonpost.com/answer-sheet/john-goodlad/goodlad-straight-talk-about-ou.html.
Venter, E. (2004). "The notion of ubuntu and communalism in African educational discourse". *Studies in Philosophy and Education*. 23, pp. 149–160.
Widener, A. (2007). "Family friendly policy: lessons from Europe Part II". *The Public Manager*. Retrieved at: http://www.aspaonline.org/global/Vol36N4_FamilyFriendly_Widener.pdf.
Yosso (2005). "Whose culture has capital? A critical race discussion of community cultural wealth". *Journal of Race and Ethnicity*. 8(1), pp. 61–91.

DOI: 10.1057/9781137351845

5

The School Environment: Common Purpose in Separate Spaces

Carly Anderson, Sarah Cole, Kevin De La Montaigne, Sheila Keefe, Mary Claire O'Donnell, Casey Quinlan, Mary Clare Rigali, and Michael Savage with Brian S Collier

Abstract: *Space and environment constitute significant parts of the school experience. In this chapter student co-authors try to understand the importance of the spatial elements of their own schooled experience while at the same time trying to place an emphasis on the importance of creating a positive classroom environment. The authors challenge the notion of passive environments by sharing their own thinking about spaces as fertile pedagogical tools. The chapter outlines the ways in which students perceive and conceive of the spaces they occupy on a daily basis as well as how they interact with each other and the spaces of their school environment. This, the authors argue, shapes the entire educational experience, and as these student-authors largely attended schools with supportive and active environments that nurtured their educational successes, one need only imagine how more threatening environments might change the equation.*

Collier, Brian S, McKenna, Maria K. and Burke, Kevin J. *College Student Voices on Educational Reform: Challenging and Changing Conversations*. New York: Palgrave Macmillan, 2013. DOI: 10.1057/9781137351845.

Foreword

This chapter, written by undergraduates with a diverse set of personal experiences, but from a common pool of those selected to attend one kind of university, discusses the school environment. As part of the nation's elect in terms of educational attainment these students think about education through the lenses of their own experiences. As a result of their experiences they think about school and schooling in very particular ways and for that reason they struggled a good bit to embrace their role as experts. We positioned them as experts because they kept expressing their incredulity at the dearth of answers to important policy questions that were raised (in the public, but particularly at campus events), but not answered. Our role in this chapter is to point out to the reader the very serious and real thoughts of these undergraduates who have not had the benefit of time or experience to see their ideas as connected to thinkers before them. Further, we work quickly here to contextualize this text that is embedded in our co-authors' experiences and in reaction to the answers they seek, but are not finding.

Kelly and Turner (2009) argue that students must feel like they have a space to belong in their schools. This seems almost self-evident to people who attended schools and immediately felt a sense of belonging; however, it is not automatically a normative equation for all students. Valenzuela (1999) shows the importance of belonging and caring for US-Mexican youth in her work, *Subtractive Schooling*, and demonstrates how not feeling cared for can have a negative impact not just on student success but on students' motivation to continue their education,, by asking, "How can I even think about going to college when getting out of high school is such a pain in the ass!" (p. 157). This experience is not limited to the youth Valenzuela studied, but is the prevalent lived experience of many American K-12 students and is why having teachers who care is so vital. The attachments students have to their families and to teachers and school make a difference in not only how they perceive their education but also in how they come to believe in their own educational efficacy (Bergin and Bergin, 2009). The need for a sense of belonging in schools thus is being increasingly studied. Often the question is how to foster a sense of classroom belonging to keep all students engaged. Noddings (2008) looks at this as a matter (or ethic) of care and stresses that the place of school must be one that nurtures and also academically challenges. Vital to consider, we think, is the very shape of the school as

DOI: 10.1057/9781137351845

it seeks to care. This chapter elucidates the ideal physical contours of a schooled environment as viewed through a lens of caring.

Caring

Ultimately our students talk a great deal about caring as they struggle with the issue of school environment. They work to speak to the physical spaces that make up educational environments because they are limited by their own educational experiences, as are most policymakers. The authors of this section face the limitations of their own lived experiences as they are in some ways bounded by their own successes in school. Since they were all good at school in some particular way—good enough to get into, and succeed at, Notre Dame—they do not have a breadth of school experience despite their volunteerism in, and their study of, schools in this singular course or as part of their minor in education, schooling, and society.

Our students are not that different from the policy analysts and thinkers they spent a school year listening to, as those policymakers, governmental figures, and analysts only have the experiences of schools they themselves have been a part of for some time. These "experts" persist in a space limited by the designs they've seen and the legislative bodies that seek their counsel.

When thinking about schools many are drawn to thinking about the schools they attended most recently, and thus this chapter has a number of examples from high school as opposed to schooling from preschool through 8th grade, though some examples of elementary and middle school made their way into these pages. Policymakers and authors also struggle to think broadly about schools in an inclusive way that blends the challenges and blessings of a one-room schoolhouse with the challenges and blessings of the 5000-student high school. In making policies it is easy to forget that some schools don't have hallways, some cafeterias are without hot food, and some administrators struggle with the bureaucracy of their local context in ways that paralyze their ability to know much of what goes on in classrooms. Our authors struggle to remember the lessons from their classes where parent involvement does not mean just being physically present and involved at the school. For the authors, mandates of absolute quiet in common spaces and metal detectors for all students do not exist outside of the pages of assigned reading

DOI: 10.1057/9781137351845

because their own schools did not have these particular accouterments of education. Our authors are (as are we) limited by the kinds of schools they have seen and the kinds of schools and students they can imagine. Imagination and scalability are also the limiting factors for policymakers, so we can not fault our students when they forget that many American students rush home to take care of siblings, parents, and others nor can we fault them for thinking that hallways are a universal truth in the American educational landscape; however, what our students recognize as paramount in the school environment is not something that is easily quantifiable, it is not something that we can base merit pay upon, teach in our training programs, nor is it something easy to interview or screen for—what our students see as the key to the school environment is caring.

While they have mushfaked their way through this section our co-authors are not short of real and salient insights, what they needed was a space to share them and perhaps this is what we all need to change in the educational system, more spaces and places to think about systems that exist and imagine what is possible.

Opening

A school is more than the walls and bricks that make up its structure. Every school is composed of a number of classrooms, lounges, offices, and other multipurpose rooms. Each room, in its own way, can be made to foster a culture of trust to aid in the learning process of all students. An ideal education does not take place inside one classroom with one teacher in isolation. A school environment must develop the whole student with the help of the whole faculty and community. When a school environment cultivates different types of interpersonal relationships in the different parts of the school itself, it encourages a strong learning culture where students are invested in their educations.

In this chapter, we explore the different parts of a school and the relationships fostered in each space. Each space, and the relationships developed there, is important in creating a positive school environment. We, the authors of this chapter, have each taken a section of the school to describe and reflect on the relationships in that space. In order to fully develop our ideas and vividly describe our sections, we have each included personal anecdotes from our own experiences. And so, the first

DOI: 10.1057/9781137351845

person narrator changes with each section. However, we felt that it would be beneficial to have perspectives from different types of schools from all over the country. In this, we hoped to illustrate that these relationships and educational spaces are universal and important.

The hallways

Hallways are easy to overlook in the grand scheme of a school building and all that goes on within it, but they play an important role in the form and function of the school. Not only do they form the pathways between individual classrooms and other parts of the school, but they also provide a valuable social space. Hallways tend to be the least rigidly organized social areas of a school, so they allow for spontaneous interactions between students. They also allow for students to have more agency when it comes to their interactions with others. Hallways allow students to walk to and from class together, meet at each other's lockers, and simply run into peers unexpectedly. One of the greatest benefits of public education is the opportunity for building social skills; learning how to handle social situations without the guidance of teachers is vital, because later in life elders and authority figures do not guide social experiences. Therefore, relatively free movement and activity in the hallways can be beneficial for students' social development and as a break from the more rigidly determined parts of a school day.

At the same time, the hallway can be the scene of rebellious and/or violent behavior, because they do tend to be less supervised than other parts of the school. Hallways are a great place for physical and verbal fighting, bullying, drug dealing, and sexual activities. Though not every school will have all of these problems on a regular basis or even at all, I personally witnessed each of these problems at least once in the hallways of my high school, which was not a particularly out-of-control or poor-quality school. Obviously, violence, drugs, and sex can impede educational attainment and create a dangerous, hostile environment for students and staff. Therefore, hallways do require some level of supervision and control from the adults in the school to protect everyone's safety and promote a healthy educational environment.

Because the hallways of a school provide important benefits but can also allow for a dangerous set of problems, the challenge that hallways pose for schools is to find a balance between allowing for spontaneity and

DOI: 10.1057/9781137351845

student-propelled social experiences while not turning the hallways into violent, crime-ridden areas. This balance will require different actions and situations in each school, because each school will have different hallway structures, school cultures, and types and levels of behavioral problems.

The administration office

"The principal's office needs to see you." These words would naturally be followed by a series of snickers, gasps, and "oohs." It did not matter what the principal needed. Even if you were receiving an award the "principal's office" was always shrouded in mystery. In my experience, it was always assumed that the principal's office equaled punishment although this was hardly the outcome in every case. Yet, I think it is important to recognize that many children associate discipline with the office spaces and the administrators who work in them. I would like to look at how the negative connotation of the principal's office impacts education. What exactly is the role of an administrator? How does the environment within the administrative offices permeate the classroom? What kind of environment fosters the best learning situation for students? To answer these questions, I would like to focus specifically on the disciplinary aspect of the administrator–student relationship.

In my small Catholic elementary school, we had very few administrators. As I moved to high school, the larger number of students implied greater need for disciplinary action and therefore the school had a larger number of administrators. The administration building (no longer just an office), for the most part, still retained its enigmatic character. My friends in high school joked that the only responsibility of the dean of students was to catch boys who had not shaved that morning or girls whose skirts were shorter than the allotted one inch above the knee. In my experience, the first interaction with administrators was focused on the topic of discipline. However, I do not believe this should be the context for the student–administrator relationship. Indeed, throughout my secondary education the initial fear I had of the dean and principal evolved into mutual respect. Over time and through interaction they transformed into adults who were helping, not restricting student achievement. This shift in viewpoint took time to develop and was encouraged by administrators that I interacted with in my extracurricular activities.

DOI: 10.1057/9781137351845

Unfortunately, this positive experience does not occur in all environments. Sometimes, as seen in Ann Arnett Ferguson's research, the mentor/teacher aspects of administration do not exist alongside the disciplinary component:

> In the course of my study it became clear that school labeling practices and the exercise of rules operated as part of a hidden curriculum to marginalize and isolate black male youth in disciplinary spaces and brand them as criminally inclined. (Ferguson, 2001)

At the Rosa Parks Elementary School where Ferguson did her work, the role of the administration is distorted. In this light, punishment is viewed as fundamentally diagnostic. Such an understanding seems to undermine the significance of administrators in an educational environment. Should not their role be more than just getting children in trouble? If punishment is not understood to have any remedial purpose, why bother with it? This leads to another question. As Ferguson discusses, should the role of education administration go so far as to determine whether a child's future includes a university classroom or jail cell?

I witness a kind of tension between two different types of administrative environments. On one hand, discipline can be overused. I believe the environment of the administration offices is influential in determining students' educational experience. Still, Ferguson's example of racism in the classroom shows the overuse of discipline. "In the public schools of Oakland, California, for example, suspensions disproportionately involved African American males" (p. 3). It is difficult to believe that repeated and unfair punishment will foster mutual respect between administrators and students. This is not limited to students who are being disciplined as they share their feelings with their classmates and influence others.

On the other hand, discipline is often not used enough as a means of developing accountability. In my experience, when students are not reprimanded initially they become less likely to take responsibility. The adage "give an inch, take a mile" is very applicable here. Similar to the environment described in the previous paragraph, this environment affects all students, not just those who are disciplined. All students very quickly perceive a lackadaisical administration that does not enforce rules. Yet, Ferguson reminds that "processes of surveillance, policing, charges, and penalties" can be dangerous for education (p. 233).

Another important area to address when examining the role of administration is parental involvement. In many schools, the administrative

DOI: 10.1057/9781137351845

offices are the parents' point of contact with the school. Whenever I had an appointment of some sort during school I would meet my parents in the office at the designated time where my mother would sign me out for the remainder of the afternoon. Similarly, if I got sick at school I would wait in the nurse's office until a parent could pick me up. Additionally, parent–teacher associations almost exclusively work with administrators. Thus, the relationship between administrators and parents is of particular importance. This begs the question: how do these relationships affect students? My strongest influences were my parents. If this is true in most cases, it seems likely that a parent's positive or negative interaction with school administrators will affect a student. The fostering of mutuality of respect then, begins with the relationships between and among the administration, parents and students.

The classroom

A lot goes on in a classroom. Teachers try to teach, students try to learn (or maybe just stay awake), tests are given, homework is turned in, friendships are made, and gossip is spread. The environment of a classroom, then, has the opportunity to foster many things, such as a love of learning among students and a respect for teaching as a profession.

Student engagement is an essential part of any classroom regardless of grade level. It is also possibly one of the most challenging aspects of teaching. How can teachers instill a passion for learning in their students? How are students motivated to do their work, study, and be interested in class material? This can be difficult especially when you consider the differences among students in a classroom as well as the external pressures schools are currently facing. There seems to be a tension between standardization and individualization within schools. On the one hand, students within a classroom can learn in different ways and will struggle with different topics. This issue seems to require a more individualized plan by the teacher in order to fully reach every student in his or her class. On the other hand, top-down policies are putting more pressure on schools and teachers to produce passing test results from their students. With high stakes testing becoming the norm, schools, administrators, and teachers have a lot to lose if they do not live up the standards set for them. This would seem to create a need for a standardized curriculum focused on test preparation. The question becomes: how do schools

DOI: 10.1057/9781137351845

prioritize engagement and passion for learning while combating the very real danger of their being shut down? I think that the culture of a school is key.

A school must communicate to its students what it values and what it expects from all constituents. And although things like mission statements and visions, borrowed from the corporate world, can seem silly and unhelpful, done correctly, a communiqué like this can create a school environment where students, teachers, and staff are all aware of their responsibilities and what their goals are. The culture of the school must also revolve around more than just grades and GPA. Classes can often be completed and passed (maybe even with an A) with little to no engagement from students. Interestingly, it seems that the lower grade levels do a better job of this focus on engagement compared to middle and high schools, where the focus tends to turn to grades and GPA. Upper grade levels could learn from elementary schools where students are still encouraged to be curious and question things often. Why that aspect of schooling is disappearing in favor of measurable outcomes at the upper levels is puzzling.

Another important aspect that occurs within the classroom encapsulates relationships between students and teachers. This relationship can greatly affect the experience of a student in a classroom. One of the most important factors of a student–teacher relationship is the teacher's involvement in the student's life. How well does a teacher know his or her students? Is the teacher available and willing to meet with parents and students? Does the teacher make an effort to learn about his or her students and their interests outside of class? Students who feel like they have a good relationship with their teacher will likely be more willing to work hard because they do not want to let down their teacher, who cares about them. A key component in this relationship, as in any relationship, is respect. Teachers require students' respect so that their authority is recognized, and students require teachers' respect so that they feel like they are an important part of their classroom. Without respect, the classroom structure fails to be supportive of student learning and often turns into an authoritarian nightmare. Structure is important, but control can stifle creativity, learning, and fun within the classroom.

Similarly, relationships between students often form within classrooms. Although class is not considered social time within the school day, there is still a lot of peer-to-peer interaction that occurs. This provides a chance for new friendships to be made, but also for bullying to

DOI: 10.1057/9781137351845

occur. The classroom has a unique dynamic because learning about content is framed within social interactions from desk to desk. It provides an opportunity for students to discuss things and grow as individuals. And the quality of this interaction will depend on the structure of the classroom; one hopes it is a space of respect, curiosity and some form of ideational interactivity.

Another important aspect within the classroom is how it connects to its outside community. This is extremely important within schools because context matters. No two schools are exactly alike or are in the exact same neighborhood and town. There will be different cultural values, different colloquial phrases and sayings, and a different history of individual schools and cities. School populations greatly vary and different languages might be spoken. Because of this, a classroom without context is not serving its students properly. Integrating context into curriculum also creates an opportunity for students to connect to the community they live in and learn more about it. Creating a culturally relevant curriculum helps students learn better and also helps them be more engaged, as the material is better related to them.

The teachers' room

In my elementary school, the teachers' room was always off limits to students. It was probably the only place in the school that we could not consider "ours." Even classrooms not our own were deemed accessible and available at all times, but the door to the teachers' room divided it from more than just the hallway.

We always wondered what happened behind the closed door, in the room where teachers flocked during our lunch and recess period, leaving the cafeteria aides and recess monitors responsible for our behavior for 40 minutes. This place, we thought, was where teachers talked about their students, their classrooms. It was difficult to comprehend that teachers would actually converse about their personal lives—as a young student, it is difficult to fathom that a teacher may actually have a life outside of the school.

At my high school, we did not actually have a teachers' room. Instead, teachers had a corner of the cafeteria understood to be theirs. This was never an issue—in high school, we wanted to be as far away as possible from our teachers at all times, and their imagined conversations were

DOI: 10.1057/9781137351845

no longer interesting. In elementary school we may have been intrigued at the opportunity to eavesdrop, but in high school, consumed by the dramas of our own lives, we were indifferent to any conversations that may have been taking place.

Teachers are the key link within the school community. They are participants in and creators of many relationships that simultaneously structure and fuel the school environment. There are teacher–teacher relationships, teacher–student relationships, teacher–administrator relationships, and teacher–parent relationships; each adds a different dimension to the school environment. These categories are not mutually exclusive, nor are they the only relationships important to the school environment. Yet they are foundational ones that permeate the school environment and allow for the creation of others.

Teacher–teacher relationships

One of the best forms of individual and team support is built from the relationships teachers have with each other. Fellow teachers are those most likely to understand the challenges and successes that teachers experience in the classroom. They are also the ones with the most relevant experiences or advice to share. What a single teacher can accomplish pales in comparison to what a team of teachers can accomplish, and therefore successful teachers take advantage of the opportunity to get to know each other both as teaching professionals and as individuals.

However, the relationships among teachers often arise solely from the initiative of the teachers themselves—there is little formal opportunity for teachers to work together outside of the classroom, but inside the school building. Some schools, including my middle school, set up teams of teachers to teach groups of students; other schools organize teachers by department or grade level, or stratify faculty in both ways. For new teachers, the opportunity to observe and gain insight from more experienced teachers can set the tone for the entire year. New teachers face considerable challenges in their first year, leading to the problems with teacher attrition that plague school systems around the country. Teachers need to feel both appreciated and supported, and the best resource for such networking comes from their co-teachers.

The teachers' room lends itself to the creation of a teacher-only community—but this community then permeates the larger school community and leads to relationships of a different nature. How teachers

DOI: 10.1057/9781137351845

treat each other sets an example for how students should treat others—as peers, friends, leaders, and teammates.

Teacher–student relationships

The impact of strong teachers on a child's learning, motivation, and educational attainment has been measured in a variety of ways, always reaching the same conclusion: well-trained, dedicated teachers achieve positive results.

The teacher role is multifaceted. While primarily an instructor, teachers also step into the role of mentor and confidant; coach and cheerleader; a parental figure who consistently demands respect and authority. The teachers who stand out in children's experiences are the ones whose roles extend beyond the classroom and traditional expectations: the teacher who takes extra time after school to help a student struggling in math, or who shows up to a baseball game where several students may be playing. When problems arise in the home—or for a student from a home where problems are constant—teachers are often expected to step up and provide greater support where the parents may be unable to do so.

Communication is key to bridge the gap between generations, and the roles of teachers and students must be clearly defined. For many students who are considered underserved or disadvantaged by contemporary research, there often exists a dearth of positive parental contact. The relationship between a teacher—who has invested not only in his or her own education, but invests in the education of others—and a student has incredible potential to fill this gap. Students are less likely to get in trouble in school when they have respect for their teachers or feel closer to them. Crosnoe, Johnson, and Elder (2004) also find that minority students, who often feel alienated from their peers, benefit most from relationships with teachers who are of the same race or ethnicity.

Strong teacher–student relationships are also formally necessary if students are to continue into higher education. Colleges require teacher recommendations, and within the college environment, professor–student relationships are necessary for recommendations and job references for post-college endeavors. Teacher–student relationships are not fostered in the teachers' room, but in the surrounding space of the school. However, the teachers' room remains integral to the formation of teacher–student relationships, because it serves as teachers' thinking space, their feedback space, and their support space as they work to establish relationships with students.

DOI: 10.1057/9781137351845

Teacher–administrator relationships

In addition to teachers and students, the administration and staff fill out the remaining school roles. The administration—namely superintendents, principles, and other leaders—are crucial support to teachers, yet they often become immersed in the technical details of running the school. The administration serves as the structural leader of a school, as opposed to the academic leader, which has forced some schools to reconsider how responsibilities are divided and led to the creation of multiple principal and dean roles within a single school building.

Administrators are often the featured adults within the school. Their relationships with students can be limited to a foundation in authority: the principal knows the students who stand out because of poor behavior or exceptional living situations. The teachers' room is not essential to the day of an administrator. The administrator may not fit in with teachers because one of the main responsibilities of the job is to oversee and rate teacher performance. This separates administrators from teachers just as students are separated from teachers. The separation—the closed door—can lead to tension between administrators and students. Theoretically, teachers and administrators are working toward the same goal—educating students—but administrators, at least at larger schools, have far less contact with students, and therefore must base their conclusions not on witnessing actual learning, but on the presentation of results.

A strong principal or superintendent sets the tone for the school environment. If teachers are motivated, they will perform better in their classroom, increasing the energy and enthusiasm of students. If teachers believe that their supervisor is supportive, positive, dedicated, and trustworthy, they will seek him or her out for advice and ideas. However, even the principals who have these skills do not necessarily have spare time, so that teachers find that turning to their teacher peers in camaraderie is the best solution. It is not that administrators are not welcome in the teachers' room—although some certainly do earn exclusion—but they often are not available to meet with teachers in addition to their other responsibilities. Teacher support, in the form of administration, must become more evident in schools, so that the school structure is not strained right from the top.

Teacher–parent relationships

A final important relationship to the school environment brings the outside in: parent–teacher relationships. Parents are enormous influences on

DOI: 10.1057/9781137351845

a child's education, from ensuring that their children make it to school on time, to packing nutritious lunches, to helping with homework. Parent presence makes a difference, and no one knows this better than teachers.

The teacher–parent relationship, while mutually beneficial, is often brought about by the teacher's initiative. Many middle and upper-middle class parents do not need to be asked to participate in their child's education: if anything many complaints are that they are overbearing in their engagement. I remember the posting of class assignments in elementary school was always a huge deal, for students and parents alike. There were parents who consistently pushed and pulled for their children to get the "best" teacher, with best being decided by the parent and not "best fit" by the administrators and teachers themselves.

The teacher–parent relationships often fades in presence and perceived importance as students get older, but it is as crucial for parents to be involved in their children's education during high school as it was during elementary school. Parents must be aware—and teachers must make them aware—but both sides need to reach out to the other in order to establish and maintain a relationship that is beneficial for students in the classroom.

The cafeteria

The cafeteria, the dining hall, the mess hall—whatever its name, almost every school has it. During the school day, lunchtime offers a chance to relax, to step back from academic pressures, to socialize and enjoy a midday break. The true environment of a place emerges in these moments of downtime. When lessons are not being taught and programs are not being run, what is the nature of interaction? Do students and faculty eat together? Do they talk together? What do they talk about? How do students behave when not directly supervised, as in a classroom? *Respect* must be the foundation for any successful community—especially a community of learning. Respect, however, is devilishly hard to measure. Perhaps "the respect quotient" of a community can be read by measuring the products of respectful culture: positive relationships.

Experts have researched and written on the value of relationships in education, and concluded that positive attachments directly influence students' school success. Bergin and Bergin (2009) have published these findings on positive relationships and student development stating that: "In this era of accountability, enhancing teacher-student relationships is not merely an add-on, but rather is fundamental to raising achievement" (p. 141). Bergin and Bergin address how "secure attachments" promote greater emotional regulation, social competence, willingness to take on challenges, as well as lower levels of ADHD and delinquency, all associated with higher achievement. The fundamental message of such research is simple: achievement does not emerge in a vacuum. Often, students are not engaged because they score well on tests, or receive recognition. They receive recognition and score well on tests precisely *because they are engaged.* Ordinary students *become* extraordinary by working hard and by being exposed to activities that go beyond the norm. A good teacher can present activities that go beyond the norm. A great teacher not only teaches material, but teaches students how to work hard and offers them an environment in which to do so. In an increasingly chaotic culture, the challenge to motivate students may be the toughest hurdle of all for educators. To motivate, without fear or bribery, requires tireless effort, indeed it requires care. Though students might work to please their teachers, they should ultimately work for *themselves*. It is good for students to study to pass the end-of-year exam; it is better for students to study because they want to learn and master the material. This type of self-motivation can only emerge when students are supported by their peers and motivated by teachers; in other words, from a foundation of *respect.*

In October 2011, two Los Angeles students—Claudia Gomez and Leslie Mendoza—published a commentary on the importance of positive school environments. They wrote:

> Graduating from high school is the dream of most L.A. students... But just getting to and staying in school can be a daily struggle, especially for those of us coming from the poorest communities. And when we arrive at campus, we often feel unwelcome and unmotivated in a climate where police and parole officers may outnumber counselors, and teacher layoffs create overcrowded classes. (p. 1)

The two students cited, "aggressive policing in and around schools, high suspension rates and a basic lack of respect for students by staff" (p. 1) as contributing to conditions which isolate and alienate the most at-risk students. Gomez and Mendoza proposed that rather than directing funding toward greater law enforcement on campuses, schools should

DOI: 10.1057/9781137351845

invest in counseling and look to models of restorative justice to resolve disciplinary issues. They conclude their article by affirming that: "In a school climate where students are treated with respect, and expectations are high, we will respond by respecting teachers and administrators and reaching our full potential" (p. 1). Students and scholars agree: a culture of respect breeds more respect and allows for the fruitful relationships that promote academic success.

School should never be boring; successful classrooms should banish boredom and embrace a sense of excitement for learning. Though different schools across the country face challenges unique to their community and culture, committing to and promoting respect is a universally attainable aim. Not all schools can maintain a small enrollment or offer elaborate and expensive programs, but all schools can promote a unifying sense of community, rooted in a commitment to core values. Any school that envisions such a culture for their students must work to create and protect it on a daily basis. In addition to the traditional goals of being prepared for class and holding high expectations, teachers should strive to increase positive interactions with students. Esquith (2007) writes that, "Any teacher who is sincere and ambitious about what he does opens himself up to colossal failures and heartbreaking disappointments" (p. 24). Indeed, talk of passion and mutual respect and lifelong love of learning may sound at best idealistic and at worst blindly naive. Yet I hope that such optimism can be reality. And I'd submit that one of the best measures of whether teachers and students value each other can be seen in the quality of interactions in the cafeteria on a daily basis.

The gymnasium and athletic facilities

Student learning in school, from kindergarten to high school, takes place both inside and outside the classroom, in and around the school building itself. In the classroom, students learn critical thinking skills, writing techniques, and the history of the world. These lessons help them become informed citizens. And no one will discount the importance of these lessons. But an important part of every education involves the student-to-student relations that are developed on athletic fields and in gymnasiums. In these arenas, students learn to interact with peers. They learn conflict resolution. They learn how to act as a team, looking out for everyone, for the good of themselves and each individual. These

DOI: 10.1057/9781137351845

important interactions help develop the whole student and should not be overlooked in school environments.

In gym class, students not only work on staying fit and getting exercise, they learn to interact with students they may not encounter in other classes. Gym classes are rarely, and should not be, divided into categories like "honors" or "standard." This integration of students of different academic capacities helps to promote interpersonal relationships. Even if these students only interact for an hour every other day, they must still work together as a team each class. These forced interactions result in important peer relationships. Studies have found that peer-to-peer relationships help contribute to the socialization of values, attitudes, and ways of perceiving the world. They also help provide a medium for children to learn to control aggressive impulses, and they contribute to the emergence of perspective-taking abilities (Johnson, 1981). Gym class helps to foster these relationships and enhance these benefits.

At my high school on the South Shore of Boston, I saw these interactions and educative experiences at work in gym class. Gym class was mandatory all four years of school, although as a varsity athlete, I only had to complete two years. In my freshman and sophomore years, my gym classes were made up both of classmates that I shared many classes with and of those I shared none with. But when placed on a team for kickball, basketball, or football, these seemingly different groups of people came together to form a cohesive unit, at least for the 58 minutes of class time. Aidan (names have been changed) and I had never met before our sophomore year, when we shared gym class first semester. We ran in very different circles and took different classes. But that semester in gym, we forged a friendship of sorts. We never saw each other outside of class, aside from the occasional passing in the halls, but once we were in that gym or out on those soccer fields, we were a team. His friendship took me outside my comfort zone. I wasn't on a team with 20 other giggling girls; I was part of a mixed group, but my interaction with Aidan helped to demonstrate that my skills on my other teams could translate into situations with more diverse groups of people.

But the development of peer relationships through athletics does not only happen in gym class. Athletic teams, especially those associated with schools, forge important social ties between students. Students with stronger social ties, according to social control theory, are less likely to commit and sustain deviant behavior (McNeal, 1995). In fact, studies show that participation in athletic extracurricular activities reduces the

DOI: 10.1057/9781137351845

probability of a student dropping out of high school by approximately 40%. And so, participation in school sports not only helps the development of students socially, but also helps keep them in school and out of detention. There is not as much diversity on an athletic team as there is in a gym class, typically, but there exist the same elements of learning to work together toward a common goal. Teammates must coordinate their efforts, their mindsets, and their training schedules to come together and work as a unified group. No one person is the most important, and teammates must learn to turn their efforts toward the good of the group. This idea of working toward the good of the group helps to foster the social ties that reduce student deviant or delinquent behavior. Most schools have repercussions for student athletes that affect their ability to participate in extramural athletics. Detention, suspension, trouble with the police often lead to ineligibility for a certain number of games, which affects the entirety of a team. One teammate's actions can hurt a whole team. Accountability to a group rather than simply oneself helps put students on the straight and narrow, keeping them out of trouble and in school.

At our school detention often meant missing after-school athletic practice. On the field hockey team, missing practice meant you could not play in the next game. Arrest or even having your name taken by the police at a party meant removal from any sports team as well as punishment from the school and law enforcement. My teammates and I had a huge stake in our success on the field. We looked out for each other in school and on the field, and we made sure each teammate made it to every practice and every game. Without one person, we were weaker, and we all understood this fact. Even outside our season, we were accountable for our actions. As a team, we owed it to each other to avoid trouble, and for the most part, each one of us lived up to the promise we made to each other.

The auditorium

The school day's over. What do those kids who have no interest in athletics do if they can't go home yet? There are other options for fulfillment in high school than sports, though they are often not as well-received. Theater. Choir. Band. Dance. These activities, along with many other types of visual and performing arts, are present in schools throughout

DOI: 10.1057/9781137351845

America. And they are often regarded as the activities in which the weird kids, the ones who feel they don't fit in the high school culture dominated by the ever-popular jocks and cheerleaders, become involved. "Theater nerds" and "band geeks" are cliques seen in almost every high school or depiction of a high school across American culture. And bullying of these different groups is just as common as depictions of the groups themselves. It is these kids who fear the hallways and the unobserved spaces within the school. However, they can always find a respite from the bullying and feelings of difference in the auditorium. This space is theirs. While it may double as a cafeteria or not have the best technical specifications, it still acts as a safe place, and one in which creativity and the arts are highly valued.

The buildings and spaces specifically relegated to the land of the arts are often set apart from the rest of the school. In my experience, the performing arts center (the PAC building) was a building frequented only by those who were in choir, band, or dance classes. This was a private space, a space separate from the pressures of academia and the athletic culture of the school. The auditorium is often a safe space for many and the rooms like it are important to all those who choose them as part of their high school experience. Indeed Pascoe (2007) notes the possibilities of this liminal space particularly for students targeted for bullying for their perceived LGBTQ status.

Bullying and the arts

Many stories of bullying, in real life and in the media, revolve around the arts and the cultures of the different arts activities. The bullying the characters experience in *Glee* are well-documented, and all occur outside of the choir room. The characters on *Glee* are said to be the losers in the school, mainly because they are in glee club. And they do represent some typically at-risk populations. Artie is in a wheelchair, Rachel is a typical musical theater geek, Santana, Kurt, and Blaine are gay, Mike and Tina are Asian nerds, and Quinn has a baby at 16. Despite these differences, the choir room is where all of these kids overcome challenges and grow into themselves.

They often overcome these challenges because of the relationships they have formed with one another. In the closed space of the auditorium these, and other real-world relationships, become stronger much more easily. The students at the fictional high school in *Glee* are told that

DOI: 10.1057/9781137351845

they must support each other, and they work to combat divisions within the group in order to face the bullying outside of the group as well as to produce the best sound they can. This is true of many performing arts groups within high school. Group cohesion is seen as integral to the group's success, and this cohesion extends beyond creating a cohesive sound. Kids are taught to rely on each other in the arts, and cliques (theater nerds, band geeks) are formed out of this dependency children in the groups feel toward one another.

Maybe this has to do with the nature of the arts in general. While performing, you really have to put yourself out there and cast all your worries aside. You have to fully commit to the art you are creating, and not worry about what someone will think of you. Indeed, the most moving parts of a play, song, or dance are those in which the performers get lost in their passion. A student playing Stanley Kowalski in *A Streetcar Named Desire* cannot be screaming "Stella!" and be profound unless he throws all his inhibitions away. This kind of acting *requires* a welcoming, non-judgmental environment. Because of this, the students in arts classes create a welcoming space for themselves and each other. It is also a closed space, further encouraging these kinds of welcoming relationships between students.

And the students are fairly alike to begin with. The arts serve to bring students who have a common interest in an activity together. In *Glee*, the students help Kurt come out of the closet and help Quinn deal with her pregnancy because they are all part of one team with a common goal: winning Nationals. The fact that they are all working toward the same goal, and all have a passion for music encourages friendship and support.

Mentorship and the arts

One of the central aspects of *Glee* is the depiction of the relationships Will Schuester has with the students in the glee club. He is constantly shown as an extremely caring adult mentor. He takes kids under his wing and helps them through their problems. He fights for them when the school is not treating them or the arts fairly. In a similar vein, art, drama, choir, band, and dance teachers across the country are more often than not a little different from the rest of the teachers in the school. They are, generally, more willing and better equipped to deal with the different types of students that become involved in arts programs.

DOI: 10.1057/9781137351845

My own choir teacher was one of the strangest men I have ever met. The metaphors he used to describe how he wanted us to sing certain passages were crazy; he wore colorful clothing and strange ties, and was extremely passionate about music. He was also one of the most approachable and welcoming members of the faculty. Through his weird metaphors and unexpected clothing, he created an environment in that music classroom that allowed people to be themselves and act in ways that may not have been accepted in other situations.

The music classroom allowed those in my choir to be themselves for at least 50 minutes of the day. While they might have to worry about fitting in during the other six hours, they always had this space, and that was extremely comforting. The environment created in spaces like auditoriums and music/art classrooms is one that is extremely welcoming to marginalized students and one that administrators should attempt to recreate elsewhere. All areas of education should strive to create an open environment in which students can be free from criticism and figure out how they learn best.

The bureaucracy

As I walked through the halls of my high school the bureaucracy of education was the hardest thing to physically see, but, conversely, was also the most apparent. When I refer to bureaucracy I am referring to the role politicians and governments play in shaping education in the United States through funding allocations. There has been a lot of upheaval and debate surrounding education policies like No Child Left Behind and Race to the Top. Well-respected academics and policymakers offer constant criticism of each other's assessment of the current "state of education" or the wide-ranging shortcomings of policy. These are discussions that need to be had, but this section focuses more on the tangible bureaucratic experiences of my schooled reality. I want to focus on the encounters I have had and how the bureaucracy of education has impacted each.

My junior year in high school I learned of my friend's story. Enrique (name changed) was born and lived in Mexico City until he was eleven years old. When he was eleven he and his mother decided to come to America. I say "come" to America because I know no better way to describe it. They did not pack their things and call a U-Haul truck to ship

DOI: 10.1057/9781137351845

them to their new residence in the United States. They did not relocate because his mom's job asked her to move to the United States. What they did was pay a couple thousand dollars to a man, pack what they could carry, and get into a truck. The truck took them to an area along the US/ Mexico border where they then walked for a few days to shelter. He then came on a bus to Chicago where he had family.

Now if Enrique were telling the story, he would go into much more detail about the smells of the truck, the crammed conditions, and the hunger pains and exhaustion he felt as he trudged through deserts and rivers. But for connection to this piece I wanted to focus more on the next chapter in Enrique's story. At this point he was an eleven-year-old boy who had come from Mexico City to a suburb of Chicago. He did not speak English, but like any pre-teen he went to school the first chance he could. Luckily, my area has a sizable Spanish speaking population so he and his mother had a somewhat pre-established social network. Still, not speaking a word of English can be challenging as regards social integration at school. In response to his isolation, Enrique formed a local street gang that consisted of his friends. As a byproduct he would skip school, steal things to re-sell, and get into fights. As you might imagine his academic achievement suffered as a result, but that doesn't mean he wasn't learning.

By high school, Enrique was knee deep in this pseudo-gangster lifestyle (I say pseudo because if you really knew Enrique like I did, you would know he was harmless). But Enrique was not ready for what high school meant. Our large public high school was more diverse than most; still, the biggest problem for Enrique was the day-to-day confrontation with rival gang members. My school did not have a gang problem like other schools in and around Chicago. There was only a problem if you were a gang member. The constant tension for Enrique was too much and within the first semester of his freshman year, Enrique was expelled for fighting. He moved to the neighboring school where he was, very soon after, expelled for fighting again. This time Enrique was sent to a juvenile corrections facility for a few months.

After his release, one of the guidance counselors at my school reached out to Enrique who was re-admitted, reformed and began to re-apply himself to the educational project of his life. He stopped fighting, started going to class, and pulled admirable grades for the rest of his high school career. I start with Enrique's story because it is a story that is often lost in the discussion of education policy, but incorporates various aspects of

DOI: 10.1057/9781137351845

life that affect a child's education. Life experience is important. Issues of poverty, culture, and hardship are not scaled into standardized test scores. Yet how can a politician in the state capital or Washington D.C. connect with students in different parts of the state or nation? Standardized tests. But for Enrique his improved scores mean so much more than funding for the school. They represent an obstacle overcome and an accomplishment. To be honest every day he doesn't get deported represents some form of educational victory from my standpoint.

Another experience that demonstrates the importance of bureaucracy involves my encounter with Andrea. I work in the Office of Admissions at the University of Notre Dame. My job is to coordinate three weekends in which two hundred talented minority students are invited to visit and experience campus. Undeniably, my job is a targeted effort to increase diversity enrollment at the university. We invite students from all four corners of the United States for the weekend. Typically these students come from some of the most competitive high schools in the country. That does not necessarily mean the students are well off. Many of them are on scholarships or attend public magnet schools.

On one such weekend, I noticed a student who was from Chicago. Being from the area, I asked her what high school she went to. I did not recognize the school she named, so I asked her if the school was new. As Pauline Lipman has described many schools are closing and new charter schools are reopening all over the city. She said her school was part of The Noble Network, a charter organization in Chicago. Because I wanted to know and because we'd spent the year discussing the de/merits of choice policies, I asked her about her school. What she liked about it. As well as, what she didn't like about it. I tried my hardest not to tip my hand. I wanted her genuine opinion. Fairly early in the conversation, she revealed that she grew up in the Wicker Park area, but "had" to move. In her very intimate and simple explanation she embodied a classic example of gentrification. To her though, gentrification meant nothing as a word. All she was concerned about was that the rent in her apartment building became too high and her working class immigrant parents couldn't afford to live there anymore. Chills ran through my spine. I was angry. It is one thing to read a book or watch a researcher reveal her study or even discuss with a professor "the implications of urban gentrification on communities of low-SES," but to hear first-hand from this student her experience was sobering. Still to her it was part of life. She continued to tell me that she still went to school near Wicker Park, but had to commute

DOI: 10.1057/9781137351845

30 minutes each way every day. When I asked her what she thought about the school, she immediately replied by saying, "they take care of me." It is important to note that she is the valedictorian and she did say that the lower achieving students become lost in the fold. She said if she went to her local Chicago Public School, however, she would not be in the same position she was in now. She would be in constant fear of gang violence. To her and her family the charter school was the answer to challenges that face minority communities throughout Chicago, but sadly, under current policies the only way her community school gains recognition is through the academic achievement of students like her. This is a classic example of the disconnect between schools and policymakers: her local school needs her (initiative, knowledge, test scores) to improve its standing, but she needs a charter school outside of her neighborhood to remain safe. And so the good students who have some social capital leave the local public schools which struggle under the weight of gang violence, poor test scores, and decreased funding.

In addition, this example demonstrates a point I think is crucial to school environment. Schools, as the hubs of communities, must cater to the needs of the community and be flexible enough to do so adequately. I am not saying that charter schools are necessarily more flexible than traditional public schools, but what I am saying is that in order for neighborhood schooling to work there must be enough innovation from local governments, parents, and faculty members to both recognize and address the changing needs of the community. Fixing schools may have less to do with the school itself and more to do with the challenges of the neighborhood surrounding the school.

My final example compares my experience to that of my sister's. We do not come from an immigrant background, rather, we come from a single-mother household. But of course, we are individuals who respond to adversity in wildly different ways. I am fueled by challenge. My sister is the opposite. She responds best to positive feedback. These variations in approach can be attributed to our differing experiences with school. In the 2nd grade my sister was diagnosed with a learning disability. When she was young she had auditory problems, so she learns best visually; she's well served by charts, diagrams and videos. As expected she struggled throughout elementary school, but a few years before middle school she switched schools. Her new school was better equipped to aid her. As she began to do better in school she developed confidence in her learning. This confidence carried over to high school where she

DOI: 10.1057/9781137351845

consistently made the honor roll. If she was not, however, given positive reinforcement in middle school she would not have gained that sense of confidence. Still, at 31 she is just now registering for her first post-secondary coursework; I had an easier time of it in school and am set to graduate from a prestigious university in a year.

This was a matter of schools responding to student needs, but it was also one of resources: given that special education programs are expensive, they are often poorly maintained and funded and/or they are over-enrolled. The work of a school, any school, is to provide care and safety for its students and this is only possible, plausible really, when schools are able to respond well to the needs of the students at hand. This, of course, is difficult to see at the macro-level of policy, but that ought not deter us from throwing all of our resources into better developing the schools that all students need in order to succeed.

Conclusion

The many parts of the school parallel the multifaceted nature of an education. The school building is divided into areas, as is the well-rounded, ideal education. An education is not complete without math and the arts, without history and the life sciences. Similarly, a school building is incomplete without a gymnasium and classrooms, without a cafeteria and administrative offices. While teachers are expected to facilitate connections between academic and enrichment spaces, hallways connect and merge the physical spaces of the school to unify the building in its common purpose.

In writing this chapter, we divided the writing so that each student took a specific part. This decision too mirrors both the design of education and the structure of the school building. There are easy and distinct divisions within education—the challenge is to overcome normalized separation in order to make education a fluid societal construct for both individuals and the greater society. Each section contains individual perspectives on the role of the specific space—but expands to analyze the function of that space and its contribution to the greater purpose of the school building. Just as a school building brings students from different experiences together each day, this chapter, project, and class have brought us together to reflect on our experiences in different school environments. Within the school environment, relationships are formed,

DOI: 10.1057/9781137351845

lessons are learned, challenges are overcome, and expectations are established to provide structure to students' educational pursuits. In students' lives having these spaces be open, healthy, and caring, we think, makes all the difference.

References

Bergin, C. and Bergin, D. (2009). "Attachment in the classroom". *Educational Psychology Review.* 21(2), pp. 141–170.

Crosnoe, R., Johnson, M. and Elder, G. (2004). "Intergenerational bonding in school: the behavioral and contextual correlates of student-teacher relationship". *Sociology of Education.* 77(1), pp. 60–81.

Esquith, R. (2007). *Teach Like Your Hair's on Fire: The Method and Madness Inside Room 56.* New York: Penguin.

Ferguson, A. A. (2001). *Bad Boys, Public Schools in the Making of Black Masculinity.* Ann Arbor: University of Michigan Press.

Gomez, C. and Mendoza, L. (October 6, 2011). "Positive school environments, not metal detectors, are the key to student success". *Eastern Group News.*

Johnson, D. W. (1981). "Student–student interaction: the neglected variable in education". *Educational Researcher.* 10(1), pp. 5–10.

Kelly, S. and Turner, J. (2009). "Rethinking the effects of classroom activity structure on the engagement of low-achieving students". *Teachers College Record.* 111(7), pp. 1665–1692.

McNeal, Jr., R. B. (1995). "Extracurricular activities and high school dropouts". *Sociology of Education.* 68, pp. 62–80.

Noddings, N. (2008). "Caring and peace education". In L. Mishra (ed.), *Encyclopedia of Peace Education* (pp. 25–32). New Delhi: APH Pub. Corp.

Pascoe, C. J. (2007). *Dude, You're a Fag: Masculinity and Sexuality in High School.* Berkeley: University of California Press.

Valenzuela, A. (1999). *Subtractive Schooling: U.S.-Mexican Youth and the Politics of Caring.* Albany: State University of New York Press.

DOI: 10.1057/9781137351845

6

Pulling Ideas Apart: Complicating the Questions

Maria K. McKenna, Brian S Collier, and Kevin Burke with Jessica Millen[1]

Abstract: *This closing chapter, rather than concluding in a traditional sense, seeks to re-engage the value of the process of a conversation about education policy. In order to provide some manner of reflexive practice, student authors are revisited. Some of the authors of previous chapters have stepped, since the inception of the project, into classrooms of their own and now face realities that felt far away and theoretical as they worked to become expert in the writing process. Other authors, those still in college, work through what it meant to work through (endure?) a conceptual shift from student to student-becoming-expert. In the end, we find that the value, not surprisingly, of this manner of work lies in the thoughtful and difficult moments of exploration into and through difficult and ongoing problems. We find, with our co-authors, that the work of making sense of the various and sundry strands of the educational policy debate, ought best engender questions and discussion over proclamations and posturing.*

Collier, Brian S, McKenna, Maria K. and Burke, Kevin J. *College Student Voices on Educational Reform: Challenging and Changing Conversations*. New York: Palgrave Macmillan, 2013. DOI: 10.1057/9781137351845.

There are no conclusions in the education debate; only ongoing reform and with it a sense of perpetual urgency. Our students told us as much. As one young woman pointed out when debriefing from our fall semester together, "There's questions that have answers and there are questions that don't have answers...I mean there's always facts but ideas and solutions can be fuzzy and that's kind of frustrating but also kind of exciting."[2] Our capacity as humans to constantly refine our individual and collective understanding of the world based on our experiences, dispositions, desires, and knowledge is exciting. In this way, education is no exception. It is heady stuff to think hard and long about what could and should be in the world. We see a good bit of this in the refinement and "sense making" work of our students about education reform in the preceding chapters but we also feel their struggle to focus on an ever-moving target. That this undertaking was difficult is, in part, what makes the whole subject of education reform so frustrating and wonderful all at once. We think our students would agree. If educational reform were only an intellectual endeavor then educational policy would be something truly intoxicating to think about, to revel in for its own sake; satisfaction would come from the debate itself. But as our students noted time and again you cannot divorce policy—or its ideological appurtenances—from lived experience. There are real children in the world who rely on real policies to impact their real lot in life. This reality is what makes educational change a compelling imperative.

Our students were (and still are) quick to point out the cross purposes grafted onto American education in our collective national identity. Questions like: "should education aim to produce workers or citizens?" and "are these really mutually exclusive goals?" or "are we missing some even bigger moral purpose of education?" became part and parcel of our experience over the course of the year. Even more important, our students began to ask, "who gets to decide what the purpose of education is?" and "why?" While we certainly do not take credit for their thinking, the latter set of questions is particularly fundamental to our work here and we welcomed conversations meant to get at the root of that "who" and "why" of schooling. That our students came to spaces *at all* in their thinking about fundamental issues in education such as this is important. As one young student told us half way through the course, "Honest to God, I don't think I knew how to think before I came to college."

Equally important is the way students and instructors alike remain constrained by our own individual world views, experiences, and

DOI: 10.1057/9781137351845

agendas regardless of whether or not we make these constraints explicit. Try as we might, we cannot divorce our own experiences which condition the imaginary scenarios of children, school grounds, and teachers we construct in our minds at times, from our theorizing. The recognition of personal biases and filters is easier for some individuals to reconcile than others. To this point, it is important that we openly acknowledge as a class that we collectively contested many of the underlying assumptions and constructions of the Forum within our work. We challenged the space (predominantly formal) and time (little) given to "getting involved" and "being passionate" as the Forum promotional materials publicly called students to do. Pseudo debates, scripted speeches with little time for interaction, and an overall lack of attention to those closest to children—teachers, parents, and school administrators—are, for us, problematic.

Likewise, the use of crisis language over the past 30 plus years in our public discourse has only served to perpetuate divisions deeply rooted in class, race, and privilege. Thus, we also challenge the notion of a full blown "crisis" in American education. Certainly, our nation can continue to improve our educational enterprise and surely we believe that as a nation we must continue to support and maintain a robust public school system that serves all children to the best of its capacity. However, the assertion that our education system is somehow worse than ever before in our history or that drastic intervention measures are necessary because of a "new crisis" is patently false. According to the US Department of Education's own data, high school graduation rates are the highest they have been in three decades. In addition, long-term trends in academic achievement in math and reading show NAEP scores rising across all age levels for all years of available data between 1971 and 2008.[3]

Still, we contested the invention of crisis in polite and traditional ways. We, the "academic experts," offered a course. The students, the "non-experts," took the course. We all chose, in effect, to "do" school in ways that felt most comfortable. Did the course become less constrained/ less traditional when we opted to propose writing a book together? Yes. Here again, though, we have an issue of degree. We could have organized a walkout or boycott of any given speaker. We could have started an on-campus "countercultural" conversation group beyond our classroom walls about education reform. We could have done any number of things in opposition to the seemingly one-sided conversation. Instead, we decided, almost unilaterally, that we would write a book as a means

DOI: 10.1057/9781137351845

of critical exploration and resistance.[4] In using our most comfortable and sheltered academic arena to stage our protest we ignored some of the more obvious and, perhaps practically speaking, simple ways to express concern over the student voice (or lack thereof) found in the Forum.

While eager to unpack their understanding (or lack thereof) of education reform, our students were most definitely reluctant travelers along the book writing path. Their concerns began with their discomfort surrounding the structure of the course and their thinking went something like this: "this writing idea is a lot of work for one-credit hour each semester" and "I don't think they even know what they want." As they came to recognize our sincerity about the nascent project and the importance of the work to us personally and professionally, their worries morphed from concerns about workload to apprehension about their lack of expertise in specific areas. They also did not want to disappoint their peers or us, as instructors. In the end, though, the most troublesome aspect of this project for some of our most vocal students was how a collectively written and published (read: permanent in the student mind) piece of work might reflect poorly on their own, individual intellectual abilities, beliefs, and/or personal, more deeply held views on education reform.

These fears—especially of their own ideas being lost in translation or being collectively labeled something they are not—are very real and might have real consequences. Many brought up questions such as, "what will people think of us as authors, especially with so little context for how and why we were writing about education?" and "I'm not going to lie—I wonder what future employers will think of this," and "you really think anyone wants to hear what we have to say on this topic?" To some degree, their worries are legitimate. The current national climate of accountability and narrowly defined notions of expertise in education encourages singular answers, oversimplified solutions, and limited outsider involvement in reform movements. Truly, especially in settings where individuals have reason to doubt the trust of colleagues, peers, or superiors it *is* risky to put forth ideas, especially uninvited ideas; moreso when those ideas represent emergent, unfinished, unpolished thinking, teetering somewhere in between reality and the ideal.

Despite these fears, we watched students voluntarily struggle with their own beliefs. Their efforts to become better informed consumers of educational research and more thoughtful producers of well thought-out

DOI: 10.1057/9781137351845

ideas are ongoing. Upon reflection about this process, one student author mused:

> *Never before (prior to college) had adults asked me to be critical of the academic work they presented in class. Textbooks and assigned readings were suddenly supposed to be critically evaluated, taken apart in search of inherent biases and assumptions. I slowly came to the gradual understanding that not everything I was taught in my K-12 education, or even in some of my college classes, was necessarily true. I learned that information and data is framed and constructed and presented in specific ways that can change how we view it. And that this is especially true in the field of education.* (J. Millen, personal communication, January 26, 2013)

If nothing more ever came of our text or our work related to the course, this statement would suffice as a testament of the significance of finding, and in some cases creating, space for deep inquiry. This space of cognizant becoming was new for our students, many of whom have never *not* been fast experts in the kinds of tasks and thinking (or not thinking) schooling demanded:

> *I was a teacher's pet; I was always very concerned with being right, knowing the right answer, and saying the right thing. School was not something that particularly challenged me; I simply deduced what the teachers wanted to hear and spit it back out at them.*

She continues,

> *When I got to college, however, that all changed. Suddenly professors (no longer mere teachers) were expecting something entirely different. They were eager to hear my own ideas. Instead of writing a book report about a book, I was supposed to write a critical evaluation of the author's choices within the text. I was assigned to write a paper using my own philosophical argument. What, I thought? I felt completely out of my element. This was no mere regurgitation of what the teacher said in class.* (J. Millen, personal communication, January 26, 2013)

From this uncomfortable and vulnerable position comes new space for knowing—knowing what it might feel like to be a child who cannot comprehend how to put the letters together to make a word or the anxiety of an adolescent on the cusp of understanding an important physics concept with real confidence. In this vulnerability, we also see the eventual realization that our collective efforts to write about education reform required a level of trust our students were leery of giving to instructors who, however well intentioned, in reality had done little to assuage their

DOI: 10.1057/9781137351845

concerns regarding their perceived lack of expertise. Finally, through their vulnerability, comes the realization that language and discourse are powerfully complex and even more so in collaborative conditions. The nature of reality, truth, and perception in education reform was front and center in thinking about the Forum events they attended and within their writing. The burden of trying to understand while simultaneously creating understanding was felt deeply by many of our students.

Our students placed their fears aside long enough to make inroads in their own personal learning and also in publicly informative ways. As time went on in the course, we listened to our co-authors' voices grow. On student commented, "They weren't raising questions as much as they were throwing answers at me in the Forum." While another student said, "at least the Forum got people talking. I went to the Forum and I don't sit around talking about education. That's kind of the point though you know, getting you to talk about it." Still a third, chimed into this exchange, "I get really frustrated when people are throwing statistics around in education sometimes without a lot of context. People can find stats on the same topic and that are contrary to each other. That's frustrating..." And another, "I felt like sometimes they (the Forum speakers) were throwing cotton candy at me and I wanted more substance." Over the course of the past year, we were also privy to late night emails with frustrated co-authors, agitated thinkers in and out of class, and small cries for help in the midst of sensemaking. As Britzman (2012) reminds us, "thinking is an experimental form of action... the ground of our capacity to construct something that has not been present in the mind prior to that moment."[5] And so, however much it might be a traditional mode of discourse, this text is our polite protest against the pre-fabricated speeches and dialogues presented as expert behavior across our nation; it is also a challenge to our readers to take action.

To be an expert, we think, one must be willing to debate, to be wrong, and to have room to change one's mind. Diane Ravitch, one of the more compelling Forum speakers, represents precisely this more complex type of expert behavior. Her public acknowledgment through her most recent speaking and writing demands that when one's thinking evolves some explanation is warranted and useful. If we thought this text was the end of our students' thinking on education we might be disappointed but we expect after an experience like this that this text is only the beginning of their thinking; it is a piece of their "experimental action." More important even than the deconstruction of ideas, we hope that this text

DOI: 10.1057/9781137351845

somehow gives students of education around the country permission (permission that we recognize they don't need but often look for none-theless) to think differently, more thoroughly, more personally, *and* more objectively about education. We know that in the case of this undertak-ing, our students' willingness to join us in writing certainly gave us the permission to think more deeply and more fully about the enterprise of educating as well.

Pulling ideas apart: complicating the questions

Insomuch as we intended to pull apart and revise our understanding of education reform in this text, we must also continue to challenge and change our understandings of related terminology as it relates to and constructs dichotomies. Truth and fiction, success and failure, real and fake, right or wrong take on different meanings depending on who is using the terms. And like the assumption of a common purpose of educa-tion, as writers, we often take for granted that everyone operates with the same understanding of these dichotomies. Here again, we are reminded of Wilson's thoughtful deconstruction of the words 'efficiency', 'equity', and 'effectiveness' and Lipman's detailed descriptions of her work with the Data and Democracy Project in unpacking the impact of neoliberal development and education policies in Chicago past the sound bites of "21st century excellence" and "choice in the name of progress" during their lectures in the spring of 2012 .[6] Lipman challenged her audience to see through the rhetoric of choice and school failure to make note of the control and coercion involved in the school choice movement for some neighborhoods, families, and children. We know words depend on the speaker and context for added meaning. We also appreciate the nuances of linguistics which allow for multiple intended meanings from a single phrase. Still, to hear Wilson describe so eloquently the possibility that the entire educational reform debate continues to be hijacked by the use of these three words (efficiency, equity, and effectiveness) is power-ful (personal communication, February 20, 2012). Wilson and Lipman remind us of the power of language and the "danger of a single story" as Adichie (2009)[7] puts it.

"The single story," Adichie notes, "creates stereotypes, and the prob-lem with stereotypes is not that they are untrue, but that they are incom-plete. They make one story become the only story." We are mindful of

DOI: 10.1057/9781137351845

this danger and hope that by bringing college student voices into the educational reform conversation we complicate the educational reform picture a bit more with new voices. We understand these voices are added to an already complex social, emotional, economic, and culturally laden enterprise, but recognize the importance of seeing an issue from multiple vantage points including those that are just developing.

Putting things together: complicating the answers

At the outset we posited this work as a project about the function of language and discourses in creating versions of the world. There is a notable simultaneity here in our critical study about the opportunities for learning about education presented via the Forum coupled with the ways we, as instructors, approached our time together with students, our writing, and especially the discursive practices we support related to education reform. We continue our analysis by turning toward some of our co-authors who have recently entered into the teaching profession for some additional insight. Their candid thinking on the discrepancies between what they "thought" teaching and education would be about as students and what the everyday reality of their worlds as practicing teachers is provides important insight on the impact that practice has on beliefs.[8]

Many of our co-authors have come to appreciate the challenging task that "change" within American schools dictates as they have assumed classrooms of their own. Daily, they struggle to live within the confines of educational policies that were made somewhere far away, for someone they don't know, by someone quite unlike the children they are teaching. These policies are dictating the students they have, the curriculum they teach, and the time they can spend on various facets of learning. Our students-cum-teachers remind us of the real and the true of teaching. In this way, we are lucky: our students have continued to let us into their world and work and we see and hear their conversations about reform continue to grow and evolve.

What exactly do these young men and women remind us of when they come back or write or call? They remind us of the midnight lesson planning, endless grading, and the children who don't just need a school that functions well but playgrounds, neighborhoods, and communities that do the same. They remind us that education is one of many spaces

DOI: 10.1057/9781137351845

of structural inequity. They bring us back to our own experiences as K-12 teachers and students. They are eyewitnesses of their particular experience and when talking with other graduates in programs around the country they are reminded that they are *not* alone but that their particular context and circumstances *are* unique. Our students also remind us there is some unfortunate universality to the language of accountability and the ever growing mandates that schools, administrators, and teachers must often comply with at the expense of relationship building, deep thinking, the arts, and recess.

Most importantly, our new teachers also remind us how necessary it is to have a strong foundation of beliefs about education to thrive as a teacher and to choose (or not choose) particular alternative programs. It is an almost-certainty that these new teachers will be brought to their knees at one point or another over the course of their teaching careers however brief. And in that moment, they will need to have a desire to get back up and know how to do so. More than getting back up though our students-cum-teachers will need to understand how they were brought to their knees in the first place. This moment of understanding cannot happen without sustained and thoughtful unpacking of the circumstances they find themselves in or without time to grow into the role of educator; an exploration many of them embraced when writing for this text.

Our teachers report realizing in very real ways that there are no control groups in education and that policy shifts most certainly end up leaving some students behind. As one student recently wrote to us, "(During our course) I came to grow passionate about learning environments.... However, now having five months of teaching under my belt, I have found more important issues to address in order to ensure the success of my students." He continues,

> *Teachers and students are the people who best know what changes would be beneficial at their respective schools. Their voices are invaluable. As a teacher, I can provide a context for how a certain reform would look in my community, and this context is essential for mapping out a successful plan. Reformers who work outside the classroom cannot do it alone.* (ND Graduate A, Class of 2012, personal communication, December 16, 2012)

Already, our former student realizes that teachers, the first responders of education, often must become pragmatists for their idealism to survive. He realizes, too, that his limited power sits in the classroom, with his students. His voice, excepting perhaps its being ensconced here, feels

DOI: 10.1057/9781137351845

much smaller in the larger educational policy debate. Generally speaking, teacher voices are not part of the larger discursive process related to education policy nor do the circumstances that many are teaching under allow for the time or energy to place personal efforts toward policy reform even if it were encouraged.

There is no question that this insider-outsider paradigm is frustrating, especially for the many young idealists Notre Dame sends out into the world. And yet, at times, our students propagate the precise insider-outsider paradigm that frustrates them so completely with their wholehearted embrace of programs that some argue incite division in education. The ever growing perception that teaching is not a real profession and education not a real discipline buoyed by alternative teaching programs that favor young, inexperienced educators over experienced and locally based teachers is one of these insider-outsider paradigms. Objective measures of "quality," namely the top tier university credentials these new teachers have, are often favored over more nuanced assessments of practice, students from schools of education, and/or local hires.[9] Continuing, the same student who lamented the fact that teachers and students do not have a voice in education reform had this to say about parents:

> *I feel as if I'm fighting against a culture of excuses... I have parents who feel the need to do everything for their children, so much so that the students take no responsibility for their schooling. Our parents don't know what they are supposed to do with their kids at times. As a teacher, I am constantly meeting with parents of struggling students.* (ND Graduate A, class of 2012, personal communication, December 16, 2012).

Here we see another example of insider-outsider (mis)understanding and this teacher's struggle to integrate theory and practice in developing an understanding of educational contexts, We know that as a student this co-author was exposed to and amenable toward different, more sympathetic ideas about parent involvement in education than are expressed here. Still, we hear a more jaded tone about what *is* and what *is not* important in education "to ensure the success of my students" (it's ambiguous how this might be measured) now that he is teaching. We hear the impact of the expectation to be a panacea for larger societal challenges in these words and the struggle for command over children and families. The pressure those first years of teaching bring to bear on our co-author's thinking makes us sympathetic to his attention to the

DOI: 10.1057/9781137351845

immediate. Our hope is with continued nurturing that this teacher and others like him move toward a more open-minded space and a more inclusive vision of what it means to educate and parent.

Our work, albeit limited, with those students who have graduated also gives us the opportunity to hear the urgency of their struggles, once again reminding us that education reform is about real children in real schools and not a hypothetical exercise. We see emails related to student achievement, high-stakes learning environments, and the conflict that this engenders in our former students and co-writers. Another student, also part of a highly competitive, national non-traditional teacher certification program writes:

> *The biggest news at our school recently was that we were awarded some top award for Title 1 schools... we average a 90% pass rate on our state tests. As a result of those high standards, the pressure was on me and the other new corps member here from day 1. It is of course a great thing to be in such a high functioning, high poverty school, yet [this] just adds to the pressure of what I'm already doing as a first year teacher.* (ND Graduate B, class of 2012, personal communication, December 11, 2012)

Here again we see the dominant, ever popular, seemingly all-important, politicized discourse of student achievement (as measured by standardized testing) filter fully into the daily mindset of this elementary schoolteacher. He continues, "In general, I'd say teaching has mostly lived up to my expectations from last year, except that it's far, far more difficult and just so unpredictable and inconsistent on a day-to-day basis." We hear the wear of only a few months of a high-pressured environment on our co-author in his words and hope from afar that he can find some respite.

There is (often) strength in numbers

From the time our students arrive at Notre Dame they are reminded that they are at a place that celebrates the notion of collective action and power via the Church, vis-à-vis their university affiliation. Students and alumni talk at length about the "Notre Dame family" and students regularly encounter (and seemingly internalize) a mantra that suggests, "This college will be one of the most powerful means for doing good in this country."[10]

DOI: 10.1057/9781137351845

As the students ready themselves to go out into the world, with anxious anticipation (conscious or not) of no longer being part of this ideologically laden collective, they realize how powerful collectives can be. We surmise this may be one reason we do see so many of our students seek out opportunities to find other co-operative organizations, like prestigious alternative teacher certification programs so many of them seek to enter upon graduation. The camaraderie and safe harbor that a collective identity provides is powerful and should not be underestimated in any critical analysis of discursive power. As faculty members, fans, and graduates of the university we work for we understand and empathize with this perspective. We also recognize the value of common purpose and communal work, otherwise, why else would we have set out to write a book with students? That said, we also recognize the dangers that "group think" can present, especially with vulnerable, newly emerging adult identities. This is largely why we set out to teach a course, and write this book, such as it is. Our hope was to find a space for some form of alternative to the intimidating discourse sponsored by the University Forum. To be clear, it is not being exposed to expertise that we find troubling. What is troubling for us, and our student co-authors, is the lack of variety, the disrespect for the expertise of practitioners and scholars of education in the selection of speakers, and the authoritative ways in which expertise and discourse were framed with little space for disagreement. Our writing here, we hope, is a mild corrective that aims to bridge the divide of emergent personal experiences and detached expertise.

One of the unintended consequences of our course is our students coming to recognize that, as Hess (1999) points out, "the collective exercise of reform has become a spinning of wheels," a milieu of "policy churn" (p. 5). We find students enjoy reading Anyon (1997), Purcell-Gates (1995), and Nespor (1997) precisely because they don't simply name problems but posit solutions, they change the discourse in what they suggest: shifts in power at the top of school systems; respect for teacher and parent input; curricular changes that invest trust in teachers and school leaders; and the explicit valuing of children's voices. The weariness of talking about education reform and naming the problem is, also in part, why our students were/are quick to latch onto many of the pragmatic programs they selected to write about for their work in the preceding chapters. Programs that make on-the-ground differences—for better and worse—in students' lives in the here and now are appealing. More than appealing, these programs are soothing. We see the work in

DOI: 10.1057/9781137351845

their writing as aimed to preserve hope and protect their idealized thinking while also trying to provide space for improving learning conditions and outcomes. Notably, all of the topics for our student-written chapters focus on student experience not larger reform possibilities.

With this frame of reference we also come to understand how it is, despite knowing all they know, that at times our co-authors oversimplify issues in this text. Our students write about and want to participate in school programs/reform ideas that have elements of community and personal attention attached to them. They want to make a difference in education in the present moment even if that doesn't mean large-scale shifts in policy or political acumen. Some might say this is short-sighted and not nearly as ambitious as what is needed to serve all children. Others would note that change is slow, incremental, and personal. As one student wrote:

> *I can use my skills and experiences to make a contribution that matters in the field of education. Surrounded by adults in our Systems class who were genuinely interested in hearing what I had to add to the conversation (on education reform) made all the difference. In the future, I want to follow the examples of these adults and help people, especially students, see that their ideas and experiences matter and deserve to be shared.* (J. Millen, personal communication, January 26, 2013)

We tend to take the view that this too, is a point on a continuum. Luckily, one of the most powerful outcomes of this writing for us as the co-instructors of the course is the possibility of ongoing discursive relationships with our co-authors. Of course, we understand that professors come and go in student lives and students move on and lose contact with academic colleagues. That said, we also recognize, especially with the power of social media and the web, the future of possibilities that exist when deep intellectual relationships are cultivated around questions of significance. In the examples throughout this chapter, our students responded quickly and earnestly to questions that we posed about their current teaching experiences and beliefs on education. With their answers came an entry point for continued, nuanced conversation about power differentials, deficit versus asset-based thinking, standards, teacher burn-out, and models of parent engagement. Here we see their (and our) thinking move beyond the content of this text. Our students are still growing; and we are still growing. Make no mistake, we realize that there is more to learn and more work to be done. Our expertise is

DOI: 10.1057/9781137351845

never complete. As Donaldo Macedo and Ana Maria Freire note in their foreword to Paulo Freire's 2005 work, *Teachers as cultural workers: letters to those who dare to teach*,

> The sharing of experiences should not be understood in psychological terms only. It invariably requires a political and ideological analysis as well. That is the sharing of ideas must always be understood within a social praxis that entails both reflection and political action.

Recently, more than six months after our course ended, one of our young co-authors led a group of students in responding to an editorial, about poverty and educational attainment, she found inaccurate and counterproductive in the campus newspaper. The published student response written collectively outside of class time but with a group of classmates, while not perfect, successfully highlighted a number of facets of early childhood development impacted by poverty with roots in our writing endeavors. More importantly, it opened up an email conversation between the original editorial author and our student. The author of the original editorial is now enrolled in one of our education courses this spring. Again, we see possibility. We recognize the conditions necessary for continued dialogue and applaud the independent thinking of our students outside of formal classroom contexts.

The truth about mushfaking

We authors, student and faculty alike, know that the ideas presented in this book are, on the whole, neither sufficient nor intensely innovative in the vast world of educational reform; and yet we continue to maintain that these pages here hold potential for all sorts of reasons. We have vivid memories of students worried about "how this would come together" and how "everyone's style would mesh" in a given piece of writing just as they stressed about the substance or finding time to "become" the authority on a given topic. What the students could not see at the time but can hopefully see now was the potential embedded within the raw honesty of their attempts at writing about education reform and the power of their willingness to share it with one another.

We don't dispute that our students were, to some degree, feigning expertise. The reader will recall our thoughts on *mushfaking* from earlier in the text. In fact, we asked them to jump into this process. We knew

DOI: 10.1057/9781137351845

that *mushfaking* was part of their process *and* part of our process. In fact, we value that aspect of this work above all else. It is through this process of not knowing and trying to know that one can become invested deeply in an idea.

As instructors, we knew full well that we were giving them more work than we should in a one-credit course. We were uncertain about how it would go or if they would engage. But we had the highest of expectations that they would try to meet the challenge. We told them to think like experts, to act like they were worthy of the task we presented them with, and to start giving themselves some credit despite some of the students taking this course as their first experience with education related discourse. We told them to challenge, create, and question. They did—give themselves some credit. They did—do some good thinking and questioning. They did—create an original piece of writing. Through these processes an honesty of thought emerges that forms the heart of the student chapters presented. Our students' thinking—thinking that is, we know at times, half finished and writing that is rough draft*ish* here and there—is an invitation. We began this concluding chapter with a nod to the "reform is never-ending" idea. Our co-authors, by way of allowing their writing to be used for this text, recognized this fact. Despite this, each gave permission to use their work for this text and so each piece becomes an open invitation of sorts—for critique, for the basis of dialogue, and for further conversation

We can't help but juxtapose this with the story recently told to us by two young middle-school aged brothers involved in another one of our university related research projects. These young men are intensely quiet with a physical posture that folds their bodies inward, making them seem even more uncomfortable than they already are in their growing adolescent bodies. Over a cup of hot chocolate one recent Saturday morning these young men described being at a school that has been labeled failing. Not just labeled failing but given a very public "F." Instead of being told to try, to learn by doing, to "fake it until you make it" as our students were in our course, these children described how at the beginning of their school year they were told by their principal of their status as an "F" school. They were told "there were a lot of 'F' students in the building" and that "they needed to work harder for her job to be secure and for the school's 'grade.'" These children, all of 13, were told "they needed to get more 'right answers' on the test or she would lose her job." The young men rounded out their story by noting "there are a lot of 'dumb kids' at

DOI: 10.1057/9781137351845

our school, a lot of 'bad' kids" recounting stories of children and teachers misbehaving (Name Withheld, personal communication, January 26, 2013). Imagine if our course had started this way. If our co-authors were told, "you non-experts, you're F material, you must write a book with us, and our jobs depend on how good someone completely outside of this class or University says it is." We have a good sense of what the book might have looked like under those circumstances.

Crisis redefined

This brings us to our final thoughts on what this text has taught us about college student voices, discursive practices, and education reform. Our students, like all students, and our teachers, like all teachers, need certain conditions to thrive in the world of education. Beyond content knowledge and pedagogical skills, students and teachers need co-operative environments to engage in the work of learning: environments where not knowing and emergent thinking are acceptable states of being; environments where there are collective as well as personal goals; environments where there is room to explore new, undeveloped ideas.

They need honesty. Our students and teachers need space for honest feedback and honest reflection: honest space where individuals have the time and incentive to read and write for the sake of learning; honest space where discourse happens over writing, in discussion groups, professional learning communities, and through critical analysis of texts. They need honest colleagues who are able to critique without fear of recrimination, who can provide suggestion without suspicion. Finally, our students and teachers need space to be joyful and happy. To recall the unfettered discovery of the preschool child and the delight in learning and doing for the sake of learning and doing rather than to meet a standard, score well on a test, or fulfill a mandated requirement.

This, in some ways, is what we see as missing from the contemporary educational debates and practices: honesty of expression, co-operative environments, and a joy-filled purpose. Messy though it may be, real education reform should stop pretending to be about a fabricated crisis that divides and polarizes schools and politicians at the expense of children. This real work must be done in context, with many voices and common vision and ought best supplant prepared speeches, decontextualized research, and "experts" who prescribe the one and only "right"

DOI: 10.1057/9781137351845

answer to all our educational maladies. Noguera (2003) notes the sad irony here: "I have found that consistently those who know the least about education end up having the most to say about what should be done" (xi). It is not that the people doing the speaking on policy reform are malevolent; rather they are simply driven by motivations which often fail to account for, well, the kids. The same could be said of the growing power of testing corporations in our current milieu. We recognize, of course, that we have our own political embeddedness and hope that the theory within the initial chapter helps ameliorate (or at least explain) the ways in which we think positionality matters for writing and reading a text like this. Still, there is a silence around the problematic motivations of reform and reformers that pervades the dialectic. Most important, as we stated in the beginning, there are real children in the world who rely on real policies to impact their real lot in life. This reality is what makes educational change a compelling imperative.

Mary Hanafin, former Irish Minister of Education and Science suggested recently that her work now has shifted in scope. In a speech directed to students and faculty she expanded:

> I want to create happy schools. A happy school is a place where the teachers are happy to teach, where the children are happy to learn, and the parents are happy to participate. If you're happy doing something then you continue to do it with greater zeal and excitement. This is the foundation that high quality schools are built on. (M. Hanafin, personal communication, October 29, 2012)

Our students, without the benefit of having heard this talk, have proposed, in this book, the same thing.

It might be the case that we face a problem of empathy in education. Because, as noted in numerous places, so much of how people think about education is tied to their own educative process, the ability to imagine across other experiences is inherently limited. This is something of a problem of framing where the experience of a schooled life comes to "mandate...what can be seen" as useful for the lives of others (Butler, 2010, p. 65). The work of sensible, holistic reform (or sensible, holistic conversations about schooling, rather) must be the difficult and harrowing process of "differentiating the cries we can hear from those we cannot, the sights we can see from those we cannot" (p. 51). Here test scores become people again and value-added might just be joy obtained.

DOI: 10.1057/9781137351845

This failure of imagination, though, is tied, we think, into a compulsion toward dangerous love. Alison (2004) proposes that much of the way we think about relating to others comes from a sense that love compels change that is always other directed, or: "My love for you means that I will like you if you become someone else" (p. 107). Missing in this model is any sense of *liking*. This compulsive sense of working toward change fails to apprehend the individual (the school, the teacher) before us as primarily likeable (and valuable) simply in their state of being. They must be changed—without a clear sense that change other than as a value itself, will bring about anything better—because that is how we learn to love.[11] The move to a new orientation toward schooling, that does not coercively reform, might need more of liking in it which could well lead to "the shape of a new story... that starts to emerge when there is a rupture in impossibility" (p. xi). This will require a collaborative move toward the "complacency" that is "able to," through a different sense of liking, "defuse someone else's place of shame" (p. 74). There is, in other words, value in fostering happiness through dialogue rather than shaming through a limited imaginary of love.

Collaboration, in teaching and—when it's unfamiliar as a process—in writing, is harder than working alone. Many of our students from this course are very strong writers, but their writing and thinking becomes muddled when they try to write collaboratively. This is a ready metaphor for the reality of educational policy: the more stakeholders, particularly when the intentions of some are misrepresented or distorted, the more difficult we find it to create workable, humane compromise. This isn't an excuse for leaving educational policy be, however. Instead, we see value in muddling through, as honestly and transparently as possible, working toward the best workable outcome. The goal here is to have as many people willing to say "yes, we can do something" working on a project as possible. Likewise, we don't need one singular educational leader but rather we need a world of shared educational collaboration that is honest, smart, and fluid.

Closing

There are "however" very large educational issues that are outside the middle-class value systems replicated in school houses across the

DOI: 10.1057/9781137351845

country, and because these values are replete with the myth of hard-work setting people free we sometimes struggle or falter to make real and lasting changes. This is a problem, again of whose purpose and for whose benefit? Education must always grapple with this issue, we hope in dialogue and would suggest, probably best, in happiness. There's nothing simplistic, nor clean, about the process of this work.

Our hope is that this view of complexity comes with an appreciation for the vast array of different perspectives that color (or cloud) our worldviews, policies, and practices. With this appreciation, we believe, comes an opportunity to look critically at pedagogy across educational environments, higher education included. We also believe that by complicating an often oversimplified set of ideas related to educational reform we provide an opportunity that opens doors to more civil discourse and a greater open appreciation of nuance. We also hope to add value to the argument that perhaps whole scale, top-down reform movements deserve a bit less credence (or at least a great deal more explication and transparency) while contextualized narratives of successful, inclusive models of educational change or intervention deserve more. In many ways, this text does not stray far from the roots of critical social theory whereby recognition of a normative ideal is philosophical and purposeful. In short, the full awareness of the importance of this exercise and what we learned as a cohort through the process has only started to coalesce.

Even our own solutions for education are limited to the things we know; we think about writing a book as part of a conversation because that is our academic training. In truth, perhaps we should have facilitated walkouts or more radical (and vulnerable) solutions to the emergent problem. Perhaps. Still, remembering that conversations are the key to long-term change seemed worthwhile and we see value in the conversations conducted here.

We give this book to you to do with what you will. We hope that it complicates thinking about expertise, the literary process, student–teacher relationships, education reform, and perhaps the roles and responsibilities of the academy as a producer of "expertise" and "experts." And we go back to work, listening for more conversations because as we said in the beginning, time marches on, education reform is surfeit, and our time here is, as is that of American children in need of educational change, short.

DOI: 10.1057/9781137351845

Notes

1 For our final chapter, we invited discussion amongst our co-authors who are recent graduates and now teachers about various facets of education policy. In addition, we asked one former student to provide extended commentary for the chapter. A senior Sociology major, Millen will join the ranks of the 2013–2014 Teach For America teaching corps.

2 Our most substantial course discussions were transcribed to further understand student thinking and provided useful context for students' writing at a later time. All quotes herein not connected to a specific citation have come from these conversations.

3 See http://nces.ed.gov/pubs2013/2013309.pdf for a full report of US graduation rates in 2009–2010 and http://nces.ed.gov/fastfacts/display.asp?id=38 for long term NAEP trends.

4 When the authors brought the idea of writing a book on educational reform to the students midway through the fall semester, there was tepid enthusiasm and legitimate skepticism. The students could neither recall nor imagine a circumstance in which this could actually happen and did not have a frame of reference for such "out of the box pedagogy."

5 See D. Britzman's 2012 interview for the Freire International Project for Critical Pedagogy. This can be found at www.vimeo.com/31747556.

6 Wilson and Lipman's lectures were, again, part of the Henkles Lecture series. This series supported by the Institute for Scholarship in the Liberal Arts was not formally associated nor approved prior to invitation to act as part of the Forum.

7 Adichie, a Nigerian novelist and noted speaker has a "TED talk" on this precise idea that can be found at: http://www.ted.com/talks/chimamanda_adichie_the_danger_of_a_single_story.html

8 Recall that the University of Notre Dame does not house an undergraduate education course of study. Instead, undergraduates passionate about education can partake in an interdisciplinary minor, Education, Schooling, and Society. This arrangement along with a heavily inculcated university-wide "culture of service" begets a large number of students interested in education but little opportunity to teach in the K-12 system without further training or certification. Alternative certification programs like Teach for America, the Alliance for Catholic Education's Service through Teaching Program, LU Choice, and Urban Teacher Corps become quite popular as a result. From our specific course, more than three quarters of those students who were seniors at the time have graduated and are in teaching related service programs. We expect this number will grow further as our younger students matriculate.

9 For an excellent narrative on the impact that alternative teacher certification programs have played on the deprofessionalization of teaching and

DOI: 10.1057/9781137351845

marginalization of minority teachers in public schools see Lisa Delpit's (2013) recent discussion in *Multiplication is for White Kids: Raising Expectations for Other People's Children*.

10 This quote is attributed to Revered Edward Sorin, C.S.C. founder, University of Notre Dame du Lac is embedded in the culture of Notre Dame and displayed literally and prominently across a variety of promotional materials for the University.

11 Fuller engagement with this move from love toward liking can be found in: Burke, K. and Greteman, A. (2013). "Toward a theory of liking". *Educational Theory*, 63(2).

References

Adichie, C. (2009). TED Global: the danger of a single story. Retrieved from: http://www.ted.com/talks/chimamanda_adichie_the_danger_of_a_single_story.ht ml

Alison, J. (2004). *On Being Liked*. London, England: Darton, Longman, and Todd Ltd.

Anyon, J. (1997). *Ghetto Schooling: A Political Economy of Urban Educational Reform*. New York: Teachers College Press.

Britzman, D. (2012). Interview with the Freire International Project for Critical Pedagogy. Retrieved from: www.vimeo.com/31747556

Burke, K. and Greteman, A. (Forthcoming). Toward a theory of liking. *Educational Theory*, 63(2).

Butler, J. (2010). *Frames of War: When Is Life Grievable?* London: Verso.

Delpit, L. (2012). *Multiplication is for White People: Raising Expectations for Other People's Children*. New York: The New Press.

Hanafin, M. (2012, October). *The Effective Teacher*. Speech presented at the Center for Research on Educational Opportunity, Notre Dame, Indiana.

Hess, F. M. (1999). *Spinning Wheels: The Politics of Urban School Reform*. Washington, DC: Brookings Institution Press.

Nespor, J. (1997). *Tangled Up in Schools*. New York: Routledge.

Noguera, P. (2003). *City Schools and The American Dream*. New York: Teachers College Press.

Purcell-Gates, V. (1995). *Other People's Words: The Cycle of Low Literacy*. Cambridge, Massachusetts: Harvard University Press.

DOI: 10.1057/9781137351845

Index

Abecedarian Project, 69
academic achievement, 107, 115
academic success, 60
academic work, 9, 10
Academy, 23
accountability, 36, 37, 39–40, 108, 113
achievement gap, 63
Adams, John, 14
Addams, Jane, 15
Adichie, C., 111
administration office, 84–6
administrator-teacher relationships, 91
Alison, J., 122
allegiance, 3
Allington, R. L., 50
Anthony, Susan B., 15
Anyon, J., 116
arts, 49–50, 96–9
assimilation, 12
athletic facilities, 94–6
auditorium, 96–9
authenticity, 8
authoritative discourse, 3–4, 7–9, 18–19, 21

Bain, K., 20–1, 25n6
Bakhtin, M., 3, 4, 18, 21, 22, 55
Bergin,, 92–3
Bergin, C., 92–3
best practices, 54, 61
book clubs, 48
Britzman, D., 3, 4, 20, 23, 55,110
bullying, 87–8, 97–8
bureaucracy, 99–103

cafeteria, 92–4
Canada, Geoffrey, 64
caring, 81–2
Catholic schools, 13
charter schools, 101–2
Chautauqua movement, 15
children
investment in, 57
socialization of, 59, 70–1
Clark, Ron, 50
classrooms, 86–8
collaboration, 122
collective action, 115–18
college, lack of preparation for, 38
colonial schools, 12–13, 14
communication skills, 70–1
Common Core movement, 38
communities, 88, 102
community-based education, 11–13
competitive reading programs, 48–9
concerted cultivation, 59
conversations, 2, 6–7
creativity, 72
crisis language, 107
critically transitive consciousness, 7
Critical Social Theory (CST), 7
critical thinking, 109

DOI: 10.1057/9781137351845

curiosity, 40–1, 43
curriculum, 6
early education, 69
national, 38
standardized, 17

Data and Democracy Project, 111
Dejoy, N., 4
diagnostic testing, 40
dialogue, 19
difficult knowledge, 20, 23
discipline, 84–5
discourse, 8
authoritative, 9, 18–19, 21
inner, 21
Mushfake, 29–32, 118–20
persuasive, 18, 22
primary, 30–1
standardized, 9
discursive relations, 9
discussions, 6–7, 16
Dolores Kohl Education Foundation, 63–4
Douglas, Frederick, 15

early childhood education, 53–76
best practices, 54
defined, 60
examples of successful, 63–8
funding of, 61
future academic success and, 60
ideal environment for, 70–3
importance of, 56, 57–9, 74
international models for, 61–2
key components of, 68–70
role of family in, 69–70, 74–5
early literacy, 33–51
education
anti-Deweyan approach to, 4
community-based, 11–12
contemporary environment for, 36–7
crisis of, 107
cross purposes of, 106
early childhood, 53–76
inequities in, 58
literacy, 33–51
local control of, 38
purpose of, 16
remedial, 38
student views on purpose of, 10–11
educational agenda, 16
education reform, 3–7, 9
19th century, 14–16
concept of, 10
debate on, 106–18, 120–3
history of, 10–16
role of teachers in, 113–14
education system, flaws in current, 59–61
effectiveness, 111
efficiency, 111
embodied students, 6
Emerson, Ralph Waldo, 15
empathy, 121
English-only movement, 17
equity, 111
Esquith, R., 51, 94
ethnic studies, 17
Europe, early childhood education in, 62
expertise, 16, 24, 108, 110, 116
extracurricular activities, 16, 46–50

factual learning, 19–20
family involvement, 58, 69–70, 74–5, 85–6
Ferguson, Ann Arnett, 85
Focus on Renewal (FOR), 63, 66–8
Forum, 2–3, 7
Foucault, M., 7, 8, 30
framing, 5–10
France, early childhood education in, 62
Freidman, Thomas, 2
Freire, Ana Maria, 118
Freire, Paulo, 7, 23, 118
Freud, S., 21

Gee, J. P., 30, 31
gentrification, 101–2
genuineness, 8

DOI: 10.1057/9781137351845

Giroux, H., 5
Glee, 97–8
The Global Health Crisis, 2
The Global Marketplace and the Common Good, 2
Goffman, E., 22
Gomez, Claudia, 93
Grandin, Temple, 56
group think, 116
gymnasium, 94–6

hallways, of schools, 83–4
Hanafin, Mary, 121
Harlem Children's Zone, 63–6
Harvard's Center on the Developing Child, 56
Head Start, 61
Hess, F. M., 116
high school diplomas, 60
high school graduation rates, 107
HighScope Perry Preschool Study, 69
high-stakes testing, *see* standardized testing
home environment, 69–70, 74–5
honesty, 120

identity, 23–4
ideological becoming, 55
ideology, 6
illiteracy, 44
Indian Schools, 12
indigenous communities, 11–12
indoctrination, 6
inner discourse, 21
insider-outsider paradigms, 114
intellectual work, 9–10
internally persuasive discourse, 4

K-12 education, 18
Katz, M., 16
Kelly, S., 80
kindergarten, 69
knowledge, 20
  difficult, 20, 23
Kozol, J., 47

language, power of, 111
Lareau, A., 59
learners, 19–21, 23
  see also students
  role of, 22
learning, 22
  factual, 19–20
  purpose of, 41
  tensions in, 21–2
learning process, 16–19
lectures, 15–16
libraries, 46–8
lifelong learning, 36–51
Lincoln, Abraham, 14
linguistics, 4
Lipman, Pauline, 101, 111
literacy
  fostering, 33–51, 57
  lack of, 35–6
literacy programs, 48–9
literature
  making come to life, 46–50
  sparking passion for, 43–6
lived experiences, 106–7
local control, 38
Lonergan, Bernard, 8
Lortie, D. C., 34
Lyceum lectures, 15

Macedo, Donaldo, 118
marketization, 7
marketplace of ideas, 6
Marxist theory, 7
maternity leave, 62
Mendoza, Leslie, 93
mentorship, 98–9
middle class parents, 59
middle-class value systems, 122–3
missions, 12
mushfaking, 29–32, 118–20

National Assessment of Educational Progress (NAEP), 35
National Center for Children in Poverty, 60
National Education Association, 69

DOI: 10.1057/9781137351845

Native peoples, 11–12
natural growth, 59
neoliberalism, 7
Nespor, J., 116
new teachers, 112–15
Noble Network, 101
No Child Left Behind (NCLB), 36–7, 99
Noddings, N., 80
Noguera, P., 121
Notre Dame Forum, 2–3, 4–5, 7

Old Deluder Satan Law, 13
one-room schoolhouses, 14
Oxford English Dictionary, 2

paradoxes, 23, 24
parental involvement, 69–70, 74–5, 85–6, 114
Parents as Teachers Curriculum (PAT), 63, 67–8
parent-teacher relationships, 91–2
Pascoe, C. J., 97
paternity leave, 62
pedagogy, 15, 16–19
peer-to-peer interactions, 87–8, 94–6
Pennycook, Alastair, 4, 9
performance, 22
performing arts center (PAC), 96–9
personal biases, 106–7
persuasive discourse, 18, 22
place, 22–4
positionality, 22–4
positive reinforcement, 102–3
power, 7, 8, 9, 18, 22, 24
preschools, *see* early childhood education
preschool teachers, 62
primary discourse, 30–1
principals, 91
prison culture, 32
privatization, 7
privilege, 24
proficiency, 35–7
public schools, funding of, 13
Purcell-Gates, Victoria, 75

Race to the Top, 36–7, 99
Ravitch, Diane, 37, 57, 110
reading
  choice of, 47
  sparking passion for, 43–6
reading proficiency, 35–6
reading to learn, 40–1
Reimagining School, 2–3, 4
Reiss, S., 22
religion, 12, 13
remedial education, 38
respect, 92, 94
restorative justice, 94
Rorty, R., 19
Ryan, Regis, 66

school choice, 111
school environment, 79–104
  administration office, 84–6
  auditorium, 96–9
  bureaucracy, 99–103
  cafeteria, 92–4
  caring and, 81–2
  classrooms, 86–8
  culture of respect in, 93–4
  gymnasium and athletic facilities, 94–6
  hallways, 83–4
  importance of positive, 92–4
  teacher-administrator relationships, 91
  teacher-parent relationships, 91–2
  teachers' rooms, 88–9, 90
  teacher-student relationships, 90
  teacher-teacher relationships, 89–90
schoolhouses, 14
school libraries, 46–8
schools
  colonial, 12–14
  funding of, 13
  of the past, 10
  re-segregation of, 47
school sports, 95–6
self-discovery, 51
self-esteem, 71
senses, 72–3

DOI: 10.1057/9781137351845

social capital, 61, 102
socialization, 59, 70–1
social reform, 15
social space, 3
socioeconomic status, 58, 59, 61
Soja, E. W., 3
Spanish missions, 12
standardized curriculum, 17
standardized discourse, 9
standardized testing, 36–40, 48, 57, 115
Stanton, Elizabeth Cady, 15
states, standardized testing by, 38
Story Bus, 64
student achievement, 107, 115
students
  see also learners
  embodied, 6
  engagement of, 5, 16, 86–7, 93
  identity of, 23–4
  indoctrination of, 6
  involvement of, 16
  lack of engagement with, 6–7
  motivation of, 20, 22, 93
  on purpose of education, 10–11
  relationships among, 87–8
  relationships between teachers and, 87, 90
  sense of belonging by, 80–1
  sparking curiosity in, 40–1
student writing, 30–1, 34–5
superintendents, 91
symposiums, 15

teachers, 13, 23
  administration and, 91
  influence of, 42–3
  new, 112–15
  policy role of, 113–14
  preschool, 62
  relationships among, 89–90
  relationships between students and, 87, 90
  relationships with parents, 91–2
  as role models for learning, 41–3
  role of, 90
teachers' rooms, 88–9, 90
teaching, principles of successful, 20–1
testing corporations, 121
test scores, 37
theater, 49–50
Third Teacher movement, 72
Thoreau, Henry David, 15
Traub, J., 37, 38
truth, 8, 9
Tuan, Y., 22–3
Turner, J., 80

undergraduate students, 4
universal public schools, 13
university, as marketplace of ideas, 4
university events, 9
University of Notre Dame, 2–3, 25n6, 115

Valenzuela, 80
Vygotsky, L., 21

Webster, Noah, 14–15
Wilder, Laura Ingalls, 14
Wilson, Suzanne, 22, 111
working class parents, 59
Worsham, L., 9–10

DOI: 10.1057/9781137351845

CPSIA information can be obtained at www.ICGtesting.com
Printed in the USA
LVOW120914020613

336468LV00002B/5/P